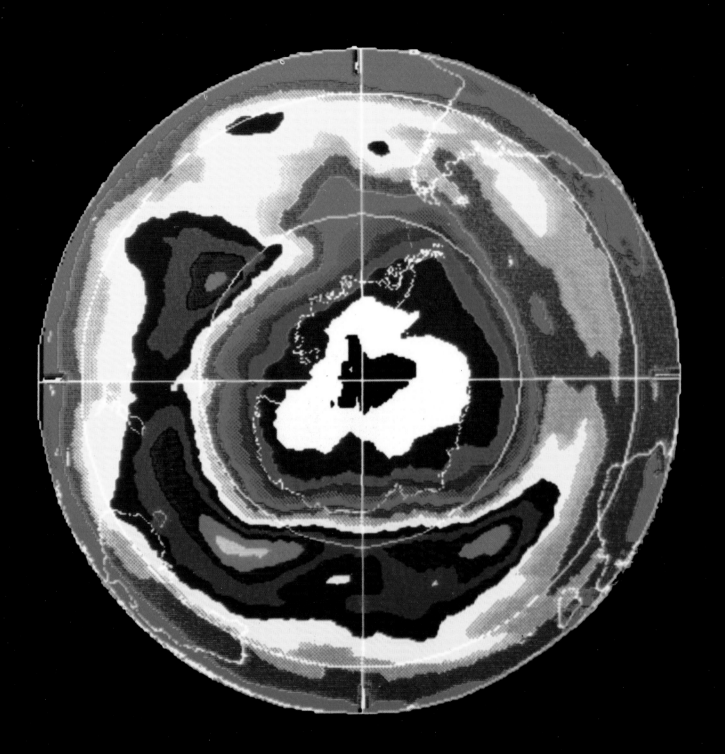

POLES APART

The Natural Worlds of the Arctic and Antarctic

Dr Jim Flegg with Eric & David Hosking

POLES APART

The Natural Worlds of the Arctic and Antarctic

PELHAM BOOKS
Stephen Greene Press

PAGE 1: **Puffin with sand-eels.**
PAGES 2–3: **Paradise Bay, Antarctica.**
THIS PICTURE: **A tornado-like waterspout cuts the evening sky.**

PELHAM BOOKS/Stephen Greene Press

Published by the Penguin Group
27 Wrights Lane, London W8 5TZ, England
Viking Penguin Inc., 40 West 23rd Street, New York, New York 10010, USA
The Stephen Greene Press Inc., 15 Muzzey Street, Lexington, Massachusetts 02173, USA,

Penguin Books Australia Ltd, Ringwood, Victoria, Australia
Penguin Books Canada Ltd, 2801 John Street, Markham, Ontario, Canada L3R 1B4
Penguin Books (NZ) Ltd, 182–190 Wairau Road, Auckland 10, New Zealand

Penguin Books Ltd, Registered Offices: Harmondsworth, Middlesex, England

First published 1990

Copyright © Dr Jim Flegg and Eric and David Hosking, 1990

Designed by Tim McPhee
Typeset by Cambridge Photosetting Services, Cambridge
Colour origination by Anglia Graphics, Bedford
Made and printed in Italy

A CIP catalogue record for this book is available from the British Library.

ISBN 0 7207 1838 4
Library of Congress Catalog Card Number: 89-63771

DEDICATION

As *Poles Apart* went to press, the death was announced of Sir Peter Scott,
deeply saddening and untimely, even at the 'respectable' age of seventy-nine.
Peter was the son of Captain Robert Falcon Scott – Scott of the Antarctic – the
polar explorer whose epic journey to the South Pole and tragic death on the
return will remain one of the most memorable episodes in the history of
mankind's exploration of his planet.

Peter Scott was the doyen of conservationists, and surely the greatest
all-round naturalist and most influential environmentalist of his time.
Our lives were touched by his. To his memory, in thanks and with respect,
we dedicate this book.

CONTENTS

PREFACE AND ACKNOWLEDGEMENTS

Few areas of the globe stimulate the imagination to the same degree as the polar regions. They have a human history that is simultaneously tragic and inspiring, and scenery that, similarly, has aspects of serene pastel beauty contrasting sharply with awe-inspiring savagery. For the biologist, ecologist and natural historian, there is even more: to marvel at the successful adaptations of the wildlife to such a harsh ecosystem, yet to wonder how evolution achieved such ends against apparently insurmountable difficulties.

Likewise, few areas of the globe could present such a breadth of fertile material for the researcher to use in augmenting his own areas of knowledge: this has been a totally fascinating book to write. Polar literature is exceptionally hard to put aside, and the ultimate problem becomes one of selection and condensation of material. I am indebted to all those who have gone before and placed on record their adventures, thoughts and science. Several particularly worthwhile general texts are noted, with thanks, in the section on Further Reading, but the full lists, summarizing months of reading, of those writers to whom I am grateful, would be impossibly long.

Eric and David Hosking have provided the majority of the stunning photographs that embellish and augment the text: as ever, it has been a pleasure to work with them towards a common goal. Roger Houghton and Hilary Foakes from Pelham Books, and Tim McPhee from Book Production Consultants have earned my gratitude for producing this book so elegantly, yet with so little harassment. Above all, I have to thank Caroline, my wife, who laboriously fought her way through the initial manuscript pages, checking, correcting and editing as she went, to produce a much improved final draft, not only free of repetition but properly punctuated and spelt. For this, and for so many other things, I am tremendously grateful.

Dr Jim Flegg
February 1990

It was after our visits to various parts of the Antarctic and Arctic that David started to formulate the idea of a book about these two regions. It seems strange that two environments so similar in many ways are in other ways so different. Why should some animals appear only at one Pole, some commute between the two, and others, which have evolved comparably, exist in both places. *Poles Apart* seems an apt title and one that immediately inspired Dr Jim Flegg to take on the task of researching and then writing this authoritative but very readable book – it has been a great pleasure to work with him.

The photographic preparation needed for a book like this has meant a lot of travelling and logistic calculation. There are many people we would like to thank but space does not permit us to mention them all. Had it not been for Lars Eric Lindblad, this book could not have been illustrated in the way it has and we cannot thank him enough. We would also like to mention Mike McDowell, the leader of the Lindblad expeditions, and Keith Shackleton who landed us safely by Zodiac rubber boats on so many remote islands; while Hasse Neilson, the ship's master, skilfully man-oeuvred the ship into many ideal spots for photography; also Dennis Puleston, an outstanding naturalist, who identified the Arctic plants. Roger Wilmshurst, Gordon Langsbury, Hannu and Irma Hautala were invaluable in their assistance on our visits to the Finnish and Norwegian Arctics. Thanks also to Roger Ennis at Bowers Motor Company for the loan of a Laika motor caravan on our second visit to Finland and to Steve Green and Graham Bound at the Falkland Islands Tourism, who were extremely helpful in arranging our tour to these lovely islands.

None of the photographs could have been taken without cameras and film, so we are very grateful indeed to Pentax UK for their help with the medium format equipment, to Olympus UK for our 35 mm apparatus and to Fuji and Kodak for the splendid colour films that went through our cameras all too quickly. The Frank Lane Picture Agency helped to find photo-graphs of the subjects we had not taken. Our gratitude also goes to the late Niall Rankin who took some splendid black and white photographs in South Georgia in the 1940s. Our sincere thanks to everyone at Pelham Books for their enthusiasm during the production of this book. But, above all, we would like to thank our wives for their support and help in so many different ways.

The Poles have always held a particular fascination for man, and have provided us with an interesting photographic project. The clear atmos-phere and diverse wildlife are a photographer's dream.

Eric and David Hosking
February 1990

1
ORIGINS

Despite the similarities evident in their spectacularly beautiful icy scenery, in their savagely harsh climate, and more recently in the epic stories of their exploration by man, the Arctic and the Antarctic are amazingly different in a great many respects – quite literally, poles apart.

In the chapters that follow, these differences – and indeed the similarities – will be summarized in some detail. All told, they make a fascinating story, with striking contrasts apparent from the very outset. Though it may be generally realized, it is worth emphasizing in this context one major difference between the polar regions. The North Pole, centre of the Arctic, is situated on a vast almost flat sheet of ice, often only a few feet thick, drifting on the surface of the Arctic ocean. On the other hand, the South Pole, centre of the Antarctic Continent, is set on an enormous rocky land mass, albeit also largely clad in ice. The Antarctic ice is generally much thicker than that of the Arctic – often several thousand feet – but this depth is equalled in the north by the ice caps and glaciers in Greenland, North America and Siberia and their off-lying islands.

Before drawing comparisons between the two polar regions, it is necessary (but unexpectedly difficult) to define 'the Arctic' and 'the Antarctic'. There are temptations to rely on the Arctic and Antarctic Circles, clearly marked in any atlas, until it is realized that these boundaries are arbitrary, set at 66°33′N and 66°33′S. They are derived from the astronomical concept of a line north (or south) of which the sun may be seen shining at midnight during the appropriate part of the 'summer' season.

Actually on the Circles themselves this event takes place only once each year, on the appropriate summer solstice, but as the traveller approaches the Poles, so the number of summer days with the 'midnight sun' phenomenon increases, until at the Poles themselves for roughly six months there is continuous daylight, potentially at least. The length of the polar night varies in mirror-

PAGES 8–9: **Icebergs in Paradise Bay, Antarctica.**

Brunnich's Guillemots flying past Coburg Island, Arctic.

image fashion. As this phenomenon depends on the angle of inclination of the earth's axis, it follows that for the six months of perpetual summer daylight enjoyed in the Arctic, the Antarctic is enduring its six months of perpetual darkness, and *vice versa*. But to return to the polar region boundaries: the midnight sun phenomenon has in itself little direct relationship to the biology and ecology of the creatures living in the area, and can thus be considered to be inadequate as a determining factor. Physical definitions, too, are difficult to apply, not least because one polar region is largely oceanic, the other continental.

For the Northern Hemisphere, a commonly-used pragmatic boundary to 'the Arctic' is the 'tree line', and this is adopted here. As it happens, in many parts of the Arctic the tree line approximates reasonably closely to the 50°F isotherm for mean July temperature. This 50°F isotherm, though a physical feature, does have obvious reflections in plant (and tree) growth, and thus on the animal life that an area can support. But to adopt the tree line as the boundary must necessarily also take account (based on the biological evidence of tree growth) of such other adverse influencing factors as altitude and proximity to salt-laden or extremely cold winds. The tree line, beyond which the Arctic begins, of course, is imprecise. Boreal forest only gradually becomes more stunted as you move northwards, grading (often patchily) first into forest-tundra and then to scrub-tundra, before the open expanses of the true tundra are reached. Such imprecision, though, has little impact on the general features of Arctic life.

In the Southern Hemisphere there is a temptation to use the boundary of the Antarctic Continent itself, but the surrounding islands, lying at various distances offshore, are so clearly part of the ecological whole that they must be included. In places the Antarctic land mass penetrates north of the Antarctic Circle (at 66°33'S), notably on the Antarctic peninsula beside the Weddell Sea. Here Graham Land pushes north like a crooked finger beckoning the island groups of the South Orkneys and the South Shetlands, lying around 62°S.

More than anything it is the richness of the seas that dominates the ecology of the Antarctic, particularly the area around and to the north of the Antarctic Convergence, where

the ice-cold waters of the circumpolar Antarctic Ocean meet the warmer seas of the South Atlantic and South Pacific. Here the oceans have lost little of their richness in food, but the climates of many of the island groups are appreciably less harsh than on the Antarctic Continent itself. This encourages a greater variety of vegetation – dominated by grasslands – which in turn encourages a greater range of animal life, particularly birds.

This climate amelioration is of course only comparative, as the mean January temperatures in the Antarctic (the equivalent of the July summer means in the Northern Hemisphere) range from 20°–30°F (thus still below freezing) along the extreme coastal margins of the Continent itself, and rise only towards *minus* 30°F in the centre! On most of the Sub-Antarctic islands, January mean temperatures range from 30°–40°F – only a few degrees above freezing.

Clearly the Sub-Antarctic islands remain harsh environments, and most are additionally so isolated as to be inhabited only by seabirds. A flexible boundary, roughly following latitude 60°S round the polar region, seems likely to give a pragmatic border defining Antarctica, particularly as this border will inevitably be largely (if not entirely) oceanic, rather than terrestrial as in the case of the Arctic.

We know little of the prehistoric origins of the Arctic region: there is no evidence other than that it has been an ocean, ringed by land

Iceberg off the Greenland coast – a massive ice sculpture but a hazard to shipping as it drifts south.

masses for aeons. The movement of those land masses, and changes in sea level (largely due to the formation or melting of ice caps) will, however, have altered the continuity of the land dramatically from time to time, particularly resulting in the formation of land bridges along which animals, including man, could migrate.

For the Antarctic the story is vastly different. At one time, the South Pole too was a geographical rather than a physical feature, set in an Antarctic Ocean. Until something of the order of 150 million years ago, the bulk of what is now the Antarctic land mass formed part of the giant ancient continent of Gondwanaland, also embracing Africa, South America, India and Australasia. Gondwanaland was set well to the north of the southern polar region, and enjoyed a wide variety of climates through the ages, spanning a range from tropical through temperate to glacial. Such was its size that were it to be in its original position today, it would cover temperate, sub-tropical and tropical regions.

At about this time, a process of 'continental drift' began. Gondwanaland fractured into several gigantic plates: Africa and Madagascar remained more or less in situ, but what we now recognize as South America drifted away, imperceptibly but remorselessly, westwards from its location under the 'bulge' of Africa. Antarctica slowly moved off south, separating from Australia and New Zealand as they drifted away to the east.

Piecing together the jigsaw of current continental shapes, matching fractured rock strata and linking fossil deposits has been one of the most fascinating sagas of scientific detective work of this century. It has helped to explain why the fossil plants and animals found in the rocks of Antarctica are related to those in South America, Africa and Australasia. The question of how such a varied wildlife achieved the 'apparently' impossible by flourishing in Antarctic climates many millions of years ago is also relatively simple to resolve when it is realized that at the time the fossils were being deposited, Antarctica rested in a far more hospitable region of the globe.

Antarctic berg – awesome in size, serene in its majesty.

Exciting and revealing though the development of the theory of continental drift has been, there remain some tantalizing, unanswered questions on the origins of Antarctica. The main question is reflected in the tremendous visual and geological contrasts between eastern and western Antarctica. The major land mass in the east is formed by the 'continental shield', a huge dome of rocks stretching back in time perhaps more than 3,000 million years, and it is this block that can be related to Gondwanaland. Its western extremity is the steep-sided line of the Trans-Antarctic mountains.

To the west of the foot of this ridge, the land underlying the ice cap is altogether different – very varied in its geology and of much more recent origins – the oldest rocks perhaps only laid down about 500 million years ago. Some parts of this conglomerate show similarities with the newer rocks of parts of South America. It would seem most likely that the current Antarctica is a composite, with the more recent western section being the result of a secondary continental drift – but quite how this took place remains a matter for conjecture. The magnitude of the convulsions of the earth's crust, be they due to volcanic activity or as the result of continental drifting and collisions, and the time scale over which they took place – thousands of millions of years – are difficult for modern man to comprehend. In much the same way, it is difficult for us to grasp just how tremendous have been the climatic changes over the same period, with the comings and goings of deserts and jungles, oceans and huge ice-caps.

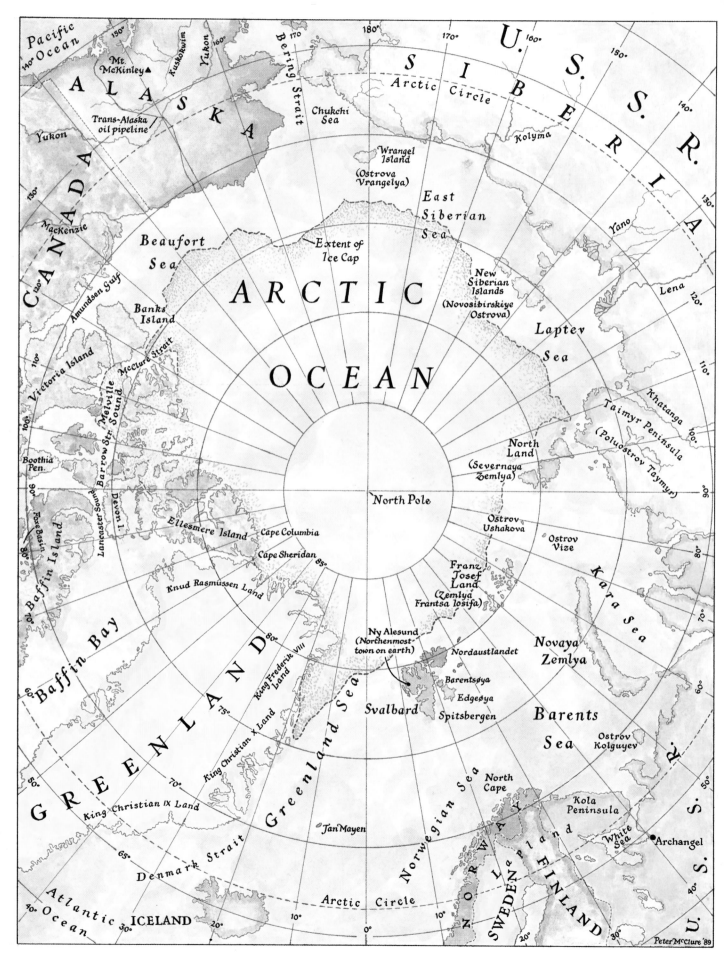

The Arctic today.

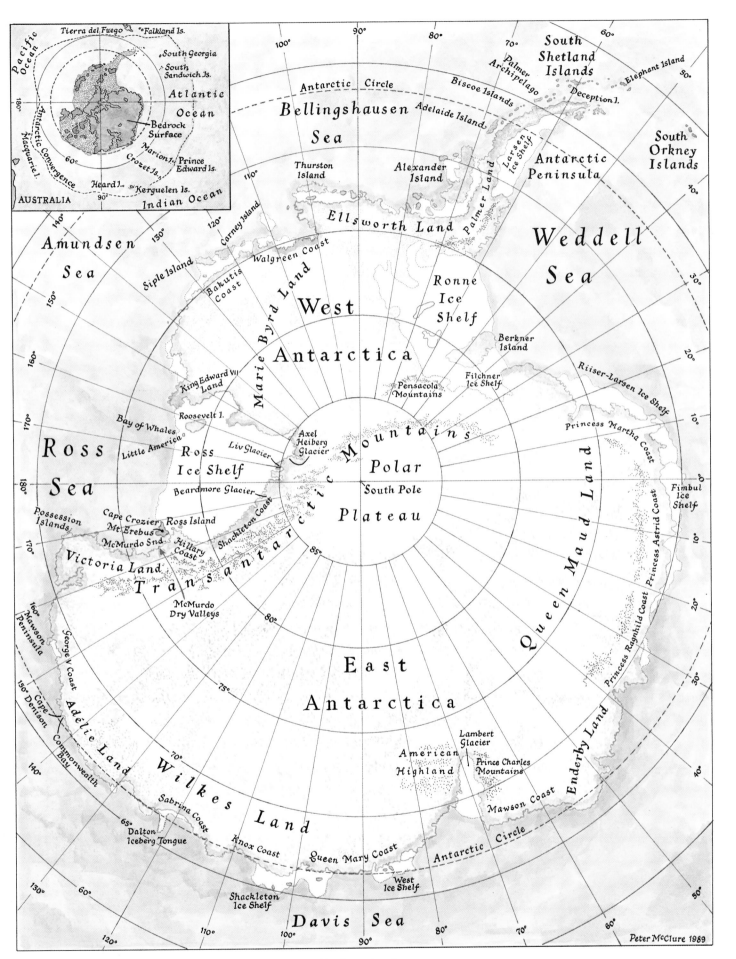

The Antarctic today.

The most recent of the severe glacial epochs in the earth's history lasted in fluctuating form for more than half a million years, and ended only as recently as about 25,000 years ago. The northern polar ice cap was the largest in the world at this time, and in its own way – as ice – locked up much of the water that would otherwise have contributed to the world's oceans. Some calculations put the difference in sea depths between that time and the present day at about 300 feet, at the depth of the big freeze. Interestingly, this lowering of the sea level did not solely contribute to the appearance of fresh areas of dry land. In some places, it is thought, whole areas collapsed or were compressed to *lower* levels under the sheer weight of the ice on top of them. But it was the appearance of land that had the greatest impact, and created the opportunity for one of the striking differences between the northern and southern polar regions – the long-term presence of man himself.

The ice cap was not continuous, as there were huge areas enjoying a somewhat milder climate – a great part of Alaska being one of the largest, it is thought. Although there were some localized ice caps (as in Greenland today), much of Alaska and north-eastern Siberia formed a relatively flat plain, often called Beringia, which, because of its milder climate and freedom from thick ice, may have been the refuge for many Arctic plants and animals during the periods of worst climatic severity. South-western Greenland, too, could have formed another such refuge, as the indications are that precipitation (largely as snow) was very small, preventing the formation of deep ice layers.

There is as yet no evidence of man in Arctic regions prior to the start of its glacial epoch. As the ice cap gradually retreated, there was a circumpolar northward migration – perhaps better described as a long-delayed return – of plants and animal species that had sought shelter further to the south. So far as mankind is concerned, this return march was initiated across Eurasia by Palaeo-Asiatic peoples, small in stature, probably dark skinned and with mongoloid features. Over much of the Old World Arctic, they have subsequently been replaced by more recent immigrants, but they still persist in north-east Siberia.

Their   ultimate   successors   in   northern

The 'midnight sun' at Ekkeroy Island in the Norwegian Varangerfjord.

Europe, the western extreme of the Old World, were called the Finno-Ugrians, represented today by the Lapps of northern Scandinavia and north-western Russia. Next to them, and occupying the huge region of the Arctic from the White Sea round to the Khatanga River, are today the Samoyeds or Nentsy. As mongoloid people, they are distinct in many ways from the Lapps, but strangely their language seems to have the same origins.

Further east still are the tundra and boreal forest lands inhabited by the Tungus-Manchurians, marauding tribes originating in China and Manchuria. These invaded much of central Arctic Siberia – the lands to either side of the Taimyr Peninsula – probably at around the time of the birth of Christ. Most recent of the invading peoples are the Yakuty, who are described as Turco-Tartars, and who swept north as nomadic horsemen, Mongol-style, as recently as the 14th century. From their original homelands on the steppes of eastern Asia, they pushed outwards to the tundra around the Kolyma River.

Thus the repopulation of the Old World

Arctic, following the retreat of the ice, roughly parallels, on a south-north axis, the history of more southerly parts of Eurasia, where the original colonists were displaced by easterly- or westerly-moving waves of more aggressive, better developed tribes. In their turn these too were replaced by more advanced and hostile peoples. However, in the north, as further south, the migrants can still be traced to their places of origin.

The basic origins of these peoples were geographically very different, and these differences persist in both language and physical appearance, though with the spread of the trappings of the 20th century (particularly those associated with travel and communication) the demarcation lines are blurring swiftly. The harsh lands in which they live have, of necessity, resulted in many common approaches to life and to survival in extremes of climate. Many of these peoples are reindeer breeders, though the techniques of the herdsmen vary in sophistication (to extremes in Lapland, where motorized one-man sledges are now the principal means of rounding up the herd). Some tribes

A Norwegian fishing boat hauls in a catch of shrimps: over-fishing threatens the food supplies of many Arctic creatures.

are nomadic in the sense that they visit the Arctic tundra pastures during the summer (much as the alpine graziers of Switzerland and Austria visit the high pasture), retreating to the slightly more sheltered boreal forest for the winter months. Others have settled year-round along the coast of the Arctic Ocean, and depend more on fishing and sealing, very much in the style of the Eskimo (or Inuit) of the New World.

In the New World Arctic, the situation generally contrasts strongly with that in the Old. The New World Arctic is inhabited solely by Eskimos or Inuit, albeit of many 'tribes' but quite distinctly a single people. Though racially speaking they can be allied to the Palaeo-Asiatics of north-east Siberia, they differ from them strikingly in culture, way of life, and most conspicuously in their language. This has no evident links with any other language, a most unusual if not unique situation. Interestingly, the development of a culture and a communication medium so distinct from all others – adjacent or distant – implies in zoological terms that the Inuit must have been in isolation, remote from contact with the rest of mankind, for (at the very least) thousands of years.

It seems most probable that the Beringian land bridge connecting the New World to the Old was passable, at intervals and for periods determined by climatic changes, for many millenia. By way of it, animals and plants, and mankind, penetrated North America and spread southwards through the Continent. Doubtless one such wave of invasion is the origin of the North American Indian tribes, who are very distinct, physically and culturally from the Inuit peoples. Between the two there remains a wary distancing that stops only slightly short of open hostility. Though the origins of the Inuit continue to be the subject more of debate than actual solution of the puzzle, popular theory has it that their origin is comparatively – and unexpectedly recent, possibly resulting from a crossing of the Bering Strait only about 6,000 years ago.

It can be argued that once they had crossed, circumstances or climatic conditions prevented any further waves of potential colonists. In the isolation that they found, the Inuit became the beneficiaries (or the victims, depending on viewpoint) of some of the most savage natural selection pressures that mankind has ever endured. From this period man emerged as master of the Arctic environment, superbly adapted both in physique and way of life to existing efficiently, effectively and evidently enjoyably in the harsh, unforgiving conditions of this part of the world.

After a period, probably of no longer than two or three thousand years – an incredibly short time for such an 'adaptation' to take place in the normally accepted biological meaning of that term – a period of expansion and colonization took place, starting, it is thought, about 4,000 years ago. Using the kayak canoe, and hooks and harpoons fashioned from bone for hunting, the Inuit spread along the coast. Some penetrated

LEFT: A lifetime of harsh climate is reflected in the weather-beaten face of a Greenland Inuit woman.

Inuit youngsters on Baffin Island. Who can tell what changes their lifetime will see in the Canadian Arctic.

Reindeer-skin tent at a
Lapp settlement at Alta,
North Norway.

which for the terrain can only be described
as phenomenal. Such a travelling capability
depended heavily on the sledge and dog
team, and on effective insulating clothing and
the ability to erect an ice house or igloo in
astonishingly quick time. Because of this
travelling ability, a culture that was surprisingly uniform across Inuit territory developed,
and was able to be maintained.

Hunting on the ice fields of the High Arctic
rendered the kayak unnecessary, so the
tribes that remained there developed a new
range of hunting techniques, mostly solitary
and demanding intense concentration and
resistance to cold. One example would be
sitting and waiting for hours with a harpoon at
a seal 'blow-hole' (used for periodic visits to
the surface to take in lungfulls of air), knowing
that the slightest noise would frighten off the
intended quarry to another hole.

Yet other groups moved inland and dis-
tanced themselves permanently from the sea,
notably the Nunamiut, hunting the various
animals of the tundra/boreal forest margins,
especially Caribou. Strangely, in no part of
the New World has the Caribou been even
semi-domesticated by the Inuit peoples, as it
has in the Old World (though under its other
name 'Reindeer'). Recently though, 'white
man' colonists from the south have been

south through Alaska to the Aleutian Islands
chain, where a separate island-based sub-
culture soon developed. Others spread
across what is now Arctic Canada, and thence
into Greenland, while a few returned across
the Bering Strait to the Asian shore, home of
their ancestors.

Adaptability would appear to have been
the Inuit's major strength, together with an
intuitive nomadism associated with the physical ability to travel long distances at speeds

Huskies: their sledge-
pulling capabilities have
played a major part in the
daily life of the Arctic,
and, a world away, in the
exploration of the
Antarctic.

The present-day United
States Antarctic base at
McMurdo Sound.

attempting to introduce such herding systems. Other tribes specialize in fish hunting, especially salmon, in the fresh-water deltas of the Yukon and Kuskokwim Rivers.

The Arctic is demonstrably not the terrain suitable for the human population censuses so beloved of administrators since biblical times. Across the whole of the Arctic region, low population densities are to be expected, not just because of the harshness of the environment but also because that environment naturally cannot be supportive of large numbers. Of the protein-rich foods only fish are abundant – and these only seasonally. Larger mammals like seals, whales and Caribou do not provide a steady food source, only a seasonally and spatially irregular series of gluts and shortages. Plant products, such as cereals and potatoes, are in nature almost non-existent, and only recently have they become available to some Arctic dwellers through the 'colonization' of northern lands by southerners seeking natural products like furs or, more important today, oil. These exploitative in-comers bring with them the support facilities necessary to maintain their home lifestyle.

Freuchen and Salomonsen, writing thirty-two years ago (in 1958) attempted some estimates that are well worth repeating here: they reckoned that at that time, the Polar Eskimos, probably the hardiest and certainly the most northerly-dwelling people on earth, numbered only some 250 individuals. Allowing for the vagaries of the seasonal movements of the peoples concerned, in and out over the 'Arctic border', they assessed the Old World Arctic human population to be about 90,000, of whom less than 2,000 were Inuit living on the Asiatic coast of the Bering Sea. For the New World, their calculations allowed for just over 50,000 Inuit (16,000 in Alaska, 23,000 in Greenland, the remainder in Canada).

Thus we have for the Arctic a grand total of some 140,000 inhabitants who can be classed as naturally native, plus a number (never large, but undoubtedly some thousands and rising) of 'southerners' ranging from explorers and scientists of a great many disciplines, to traders. Perhaps many of them are now more concerned with exploiting the Arctic ecosystem than understanding it. Certainly the trappings of 'civilization' that they have introduced have dramatically altered the Eskimo way of life. It can be argued that the introduction of the rifle, the 'skidoo' and other uses of the internal combustion engine, of electric power and lighting, of processed foods, have all helped Eskimo culture into the 20th century. It is just as arguable that this culture should have been *protected* from the 20th

century and the problems that it has brought in the shape of diseases, alcohol abuse and the like.

As for the Antarctic, there too are teams of explorers and scientists from many northern nations, now numbering thousands but all entirely dependent on the outside world and its technology for survival. The natural population is, and always has been, nil. The contrast is a striking and fascinating one, above all drawing attention to the marvellous ability of the Inuit peoples that allows them to overcome the savagery of their Arctic environment.

In one way it is fascinating, in another frightening, that modern man shows signs of being able to unlock, albeit inadvertently, some of these water stocks currently frozen solid as the ice of the two polar regions. Featuring prominently in current climatological and ecological journals is the 'greenhouse effect', an overall warming of the earth's climate. Since the start of the Industrial Revolution, the earth's atmospheric carbon dioxide (CO_2) concentration has risen by about 25 per cent. This rise has two major causes. The first (and the more obvious) is the rapid increase in the burning of fossil fuels, coal and oil, to provide power for these industries and the heat and light that are today part of normal life for almost everyone. The second, less obvious and perhaps with deeper long-term implications, is the destruction for various purposes of a substantial proportion of the world's forests. Carbon dioxide is essential for plant growth, and these massive areas of forest need huge quantities of CO_2, which then becomes locked up in the growing trees.

But what have heavy industry and tropical forests to do with the polar ice-cap? The answer is sombre. Ever-increasing quantities of CO_2 are being produced by modern man, but with the destruction of the world's forests, ever-diminishing quantities are being removed from the atmosphere to be used in forest growth. In consequence, atmospheric CO_2 concentrations continue to rise, with the prediction that the present level will double within the next hundred years. Concern is aroused because this CO_2 will have a significant impact on the world's climate. Atmospheric CO_2 is more or less transparent to

Like milk bottles on shelves, Brunnich's Guillemots line their nesting ledges on Coburg Island.

incoming, warming, solar radiation (which is primarily short-wave), but absorbs much of the long-wave back- (or reflected) radiation from the earth. So similar is this situation to that used in greenhouses to provide a plant-growing environment warmer than outside that it has been dubbed the 'greenhouse effect'. Climatologists now predict an overall global warming due to a rise in average temperatures of perhaps 20 per cent by the middle of the next century.

Couple this with what is popularly described as a 'hole' in the ozone layer, and there arises a recipe for potential global problems, if not possible disasters. The ozone layer is yet another protective sector of the earth's atmosphere, which has been and is being damaged by some of the supposedly largely inert gaseous propellants used for many years (and *still* used far too widely) in aerosol sprays of all descriptions. The major 'hole' so far detected in this insulating ozone layer is centred over Antarctica. (See illustrations on endpapers.)

The Lemaire Channel, Antarctica.

If the warming process continues unchecked and the hole continues to expand, the implications must be serious, not just for the polar regions, but *also* for the rest of the globe.

It has been calculated that with ice covering almost all of Antarctica's 14 million square kilometre-area, there is within the 30 million cubic kilometres of the ice-cap over 60 per cent of the world stock of fresh water. Estimates vary greatly as to the amount of this ice that might thaw in any climatic amelioration, and on the implications of any appreciable thaw so far as a rise in sea level is concerned. There have been 'worst-scenario' suggestions that sea levels might rise by perhaps as much as 50 to 100 metres, and the resulting inundation would cause massive destruction and severely disrupt civilization as we know it.

2

THE NORTHWEST PASSAGE AND BEYOND

The written record of man's exploration of the Arctic opens, amazingly, as early as 325 BC, when a Greek explorer, Pytheas, sailed north from Britain in search of a land already known as 'Thule'. Most of his contemporaries adhered to the strict Roman view that voyaging north was impossible because of an unbroken sheet of ice, but Pytheas certainly penetrated far enough north to encounter and record the nightless mid-summer Arctic days.

At the start of the Dark Ages, once Roman influence had faded, various European nations began to press northwards. Unspectacular amongst them, but conspicuous in their sailing achievements (which may not yet be fully appreciated) were the Irish monks, who seeking solitude for religious contemplation, found it in Iceland in about AD 770.

Much more spectacular were the Norsemen, rowing and sailing in their famous and extremely seaworthy longboats out of Norway, Sweden and Denmark. These 'Vikings' were ferocious and voracious, and in consequence their voyages left physical marks on the shores that they touched. They were also magnificently adventurous, and had a well-developed tradition of relating and recording their exploits in the sagas, which have provided much useful detail for modern historians. They were the first to settle a proper colony in Iceland, in the late 800s, and it was a storm-blown boatload of intending settlers led by Gunnbjorn who missed Iceland altogether and were driven on by the wind to discover Greenland in about 900. They returned to Iceland with a detailed account of the potential benefits of this new colony.

Such were the seafaring hazards that it was not until almost a century later that Eric the Red retraced Gunnbjorn's voyage and founded a settlement on Greenland's southern tip, the site of the present-day Eriksey. At that time the climate of Greenland was clearly much blander than it is today. The abundance of seabirds, fish and whales that Eric the Red found as an immensely valuable food source is indeed still present today, but the land surface he records differs so much that it is hard to imagine. Accounts from that time give a picture of grass-covered hills and plains, with tree and scrub cover of rich juniper and willows – hence 'Green' land.

During the summer months, the early set-tlers found ample grazing for their stock, and were able – apparently without difficulty – to raise crops of vegetables. Today's stark, largely ice-covered landscape presents a much harsher picture, indicative of an appreciable climatic cooling over the intervening centuries. From the first settlements, colonists established villages at the heads of many fjords, farming and fishing through the long summer days and storing enough food and fuel to survive the winters in apparent comfort. Christianity had reached the island, which had its own bishop, and a flourishing trade was established with the Eskimos, or Inuit. The colony was so well established that it voted to join Norway as a Crown colony in 1261. But it is evident that soon after this the climate began to cool. Supply vessels from Norway became increasingly rare visitors, depriving the islanders of basic items like salt and iron tools. Around a century later the Viking colonies had died out or departed.

The next phase in Arctic exploration owes much to the wealth of the Orient, in terms of fine cloths, spices, porcelain and precious stones. The predominance, and hostility, of Moslems in much of Asia was a major bar to Christian European traders seeking such worthwhile goods to present to a home market developing rapidly in affluence and in its taste for luxuries, but the lure of this wealth was a powerful stimulus to the sailors of the time. During the late 1500s, two countries – Spain and Portugal – dominated world trade – which was largely carried out by boat – with the newly-discovered Americas, with India, and with the Far East, especially Cathay (or China). A northerly 'short-cut' sea-route to the Far East would solve many problems and give a competitive edge, particularly to London traders, who thus were ready, willing and able to finance exploratory voyages to see if such a sea-route was feasible. This began the protracted story of the search for the Northwest Passage.

The first attempt in 1497 by John Cabot (who was himself an Italian, but funded from London) failed to find any inkling of the Northwest Passage to Cathay as Cabot searched the Newfoundland coast. A few years later a more extensive search led by the Portuguese Corte-Real was no more successful. Exploration attempts became more formalised by 1551, when in London the Company of Merchant Adventurers was formed and commis-

PAGES 26–27: **Lillehook Fjord, North Norway.**

LEFT: **Map of the Arctic region** c. 1920.

sioned Sir Hugh Willoughby as commander of its first expedition, with Richard Chancellor as his navigator.

They set off in May 1553. On the voyage north stormy weather separated the two ships. Willoughby eventually landed on the coast of what is now Lapland, but he and his men succumbed to the then prevalent pestilence of long-distance voyages, scurvy. Chancellor and his crew in the other ship survived, and sailed on through the next summer, making landfall near to a town that has developed today into Archangel. Here Chancellor established fruitful contact in 1554 with the Russian Tsar, Ivan the Terrible, which led to the foundation of the Muscovy Company and the establishment of regular trade between England and Russia.

With the same unexplained but quite uncanny accuracy that his globe portrayed in showing the Antarctic as a land mass, the French geographer Le Testu (in a 1555 atlas) depicted the Arctic as a polar sea. But there were arguments as to where routes to the Orient might be blocked by land masses. Mercator, for example, in his 1569 world map placed a large land mass obstructing easterly routes through the polar sea, but gave a clear indication that westerly ones held more promise. As a result, the main exploratory drive was towards the Northwest Passage, starting in 1576 with Sir Martin Frobisher. Though Frobisher set sail with much courtly panoply and returned with a chart showing a clear, wide channel – the 'Frobisher Straightes' – leading to Cathay, this was illusory as he had in fact only discovered the entrance to what is now called Frobisher Bay on Baffin Island, which is naturally landlocked. Many, many years were to elapse and numerous tragedies were to befall intrepid explorers before the elusive geography of the area was properly understood.

Frobisher, though, did make one of the earliest properly recorded encounters with the Eskimos. He encountered a small group of skin-covered kayaks, each carrying a man of clearly mongoloid or oriental features, proof positive (he felt) that the distant shore was indeed that of Asia! One of the men was captured and brought to London as proof of his discovery, but this evidence was sadly short-lived, as the Inuit was quickly overcome by the European cold viruses that he encountered for the first time.

Frobisher was also unlucky with some of the other discoveries he brought home. From Baffin Island he had brought some rocks containing 'gold', and this stimulated the City of London merchant bankers to fund a second expedition in 1577, which returned with 200 tons of ore. The next year Frobisher returned again with fifteen boatloads of potential colonists, mostly miners enthusiastic about the possibilities of striking gold. Not only was the attempt at colonising Baffin Island a failure, largely due to the appalling weather, but when the storm-battered Frobisher fleet returned home, it was to discover that the 'gold' was in fact iron pyrites, not for nothing nicknamed 'fool's gold'.

Frobisher was succeeded by another Englishman, John Davis, who in three voyages charted much of the Greenland coast in considerable detail, and penetrated well into Baffin Bay before the ice closed in and prevented further progress. Towards the end of the 16th century, the Dutch, and in particular William Barents, joined these exploratory forays, discovering in the process West Spitzbergen (Svalbard). As Barents approached Novaya Zemlya, his ship became trapped in the ice and was crushed and damaged so severely that he abandoned it and sought refuge on the coast. Here he and his crew built a rough cabin from the wreckage of their vessel, and managed under extreme privation to endure the winter. In June 1597 they filled the ship's boats – still intact – with clothing and such food as remained and set course for the Kola Peninsula and safety. This they reached after a journey remarkable for the tenacity and seafaring skills of the men. Sadly, Barents himself died on the way.

The commercial pressure to find a northwest passage persisted. In 1610 merchant funding sent Henry Hudson round the southern tips of Greenland and Baffin Island into what are now known as the Hudson Straits and Hudson's Bay. In 1615, William Baffin came 'so near yet so far' from opening the north-westerly route: in the *Discovery* he sailed far to the north along Greenland's west coast. Forced by the ice to turn south again at Ellesmere Island, he probed the entrance to Lancaster Sound at the northern tip of Baffin Island. There again, accumulating ice forced him to head south, but had he been able to pass through the Sound, he could have reached the Beaufort Sea, and then with good

Pack ice in Grice Fjord, Ellesmere Island.

fortune and fair weather have passed through the Bering Straits into the North Pacific – and Cathay. This ultimate goal was not to be achieved for almost another three centuries – a great tribute to Baffin's navigational skills and seamanship.

By far the most impressive achievement of this extended intermission was the charting of the north coast of Russia and Siberia. This was achieved by a massive expedition funded by Tsar Peter the Great and led by the Danish explorer Vitus Bering. From concept to completion in 1741, the exploration took seventeen years and resulted in detailed maps and charts of the Kamchatka Peninsula and the Russian coast of the Bering Strait, where Bering penetrated north just to the Arctic Circle and within sight of the Beaufort Sea. Bering crossed the Strait that now bears his name and landed in Alaska, establishing contacts with the Inuit. The contacts were quickly taken up and extended by Russian seafarers and merchants, who were within a few years trading along the American west coast as far south as modern San Francisco.

The arrival of the 19th century saw the start of yet another adventurous age of Arctic exploration – by land and sea. Stimulated by Russia's obviously fast-increasing trade and influence, the British government actually offered a reward for the discovery of a northwest passage, the challenge immediately being taken up by the British navy. The first attempt was made by the *Isabella* and the *Alexander*, commanded by Sir John Ross with Edward Parry as his lieutenant. Ross actually got his ships into Lancaster Sound, north of Baffin Island, but claimed that the Sound led only into a landlocked bay backed by a range of hills that Ross named the 'Croker Mountains'. He returned to England, where his interpretation of the geography was challenged, not least by Parry and other crew members. The acrimonious dispute that developed hastened the mounting of a second British naval expedition, with Parry commanding the *Hekla* and the *Griper*. They reached Lancaster Sound in August 1819, and finding their route unencumbered by the distant Croker Mountains, pressed on into the Barrow Strait.

Unhindered by ice, the *Hekla* and the *Griper* sailed up Melville Sound, passing 110° west of Greenwich and thereby earning the handsome reward offered by Parliament a year earlier for achieving this longitude. Soon after, their luck changed when impenetrable ice blocked further westward progress, and the two ships put into a sheltered bay to ride out the Arctic winter, which they achieved in a remarkably businesslike and successful way. After almost two months of total darkness, health and spirits were in good fettle as spring arrived, closely followed by summer. But throughout the summer of 1820, ice prohi-

bited further westward progress, and the *Hekla* and the *Griper* returned to England.

Over the next few years, Parry made several further attempts at a north-west passage, trying routes to the south of Baffin Island and into the Foxe Basin, and between Baffin Island and Somerset Island, each to little avail. Intrepid as ever, in 1827 Parry turned his hand to overland exploration, setting out with small boats that he sailed where possible and dragged over the ice where not. By late July, he and his men had got to within about 500 miles of the Pole at 82° 45′N, a northward penetration that was to remain unbeaten for almost fifty years.

In 1828, Ross rejoined the competition and set off on a further attempt at a north-west passage, with his nephew James Clark Ross, in the steam-assisted *Victory*. The elder Ross

Appropriately named, the Arctic Tern.

has left fascinating watercolour sketches showing the detail of Arctic exploration of the time, and of the Inuit peoples that they encountered. The younger Ross secured for himself a place in the annals of Arctic exploration by locating, after a series of 'overland' expeditions, the North Magnetic Pole on the Boothia Peninsula. In its entirety, the expedition was a long one, the men aboard the *Victory* enduring three successive winters locked fast in the ice before abandoning their ship and returning hazardously to Britain, having been rescued from smaller boats by a whaler.

For much of the next half-century, Arctic exploration was marked by tragedies rather than by successes. Firstly, Sir John Franklin set out from England in Ross's well-proven ships the *Erebus* and the *Terror*, seeking the elusive Northwest Passage. In 1847, two years after his departure, nothing had been heard of Franklin – his expedition had vanished apparently without trace. A series of rescue missions contributed considerably to the collective knowledge of the maze of islands and the labyrinth of channels between the Beaufort Sea and Baffin Bay, but did not result in the discovery of a clear north-west passage. Nor was there much evidence of Franklin's fate, other than a few personal possessions found in Eskimo hands. Lady Jane Franklin raised the funds to mount a further search, starting from Aberdeen in 1857, led by Leopold McClintock, who had been involved in earlier searches under Ross's command. Their vessel, once again steam-assisted, was the *Fox*.

During the summer of 1859, sledge parties led by McClintock and Lieutenant Hobson found substantial traces of the Franklin expedition in various places on King William Island, including an abandoned ship's boat attached to a sledge. Beside a cairn nearby were medical apparatus and living equipment, and a sealed canister containing the record that the *Erebus* and the *Terror* had been abandoned on 28 May 1847, after over-wintering on Beechey Island at 74° 43'N. Another note had been added on 25 April 1848 – almost a year later – registering the deaths of twenty-four of the men, including Sir John Franklin, during the intervening year. Also recorded was the intention of Crozier, now in command of the expedition, to head 'tomorrow' for Back's River (the Great Fish River). Quite why Franklin, and later Crozier, had elected to drag with them such a tremendous weight of equipment (some of it, like the heavy tools and the ship's plate and cutlery, surely not necessary in circumstances of such extreme peril) remains a mystery. As do the remaining details of Franklin's expedition.

Charles Hall, an American, set out on a five-year, one-man expedition on foot in 1864, aiming to find out more by living with the local people. Many of the Inuit that he encountered had relics of the Franklin expedition, but otherwise he could only record the fact that the King William's Land Eskimos were far from helpful – indeed some admitted to him that they had abandoned Crozier and his men, leaving them to die of starvation. Mystery did not just surround the deaths of Franklin and his crew. On a later voyage, in 1871, Hall himself died of an unknown illness and was buried in the Arctic he loved. His body (well preserved in frozen Arctic soil) was disinterred for autopsy a century later, the result confirming that Hall had been poisoned, presumably by one or more of his crew, though for what reason remains yet another mystery.

On another front, relics of a previous expedition were to provide an important stimulus to another individual in the renewed quest to become the first man to reach the North Pole. In 1879 the *Jeanette*, commanded by Lieutenant de Long, set out from San Francisco on the western seaboard of the U.S.A. in an attempt to penetrate the Northwest Passage from the Pacific Ocean end. Passing through the Bering Strait from the Bering Sea into the Arctic Ocean, the *Jeanette* became trapped in the ice and drifted past Wrangle Island to the New Siberian Islands. Here she was crushed and destroyed, but a few of her crew were able to reach safety in Siberia. Three years later, wreckage and seamen's oilskins from the *Jeanette* were washed ashore on the south-west coast of Greenland, immediately triggering conjecture as to which route was followed and under the influence of which currents this improbable journey was achieved.

One of those whose imagination was fired by the incident was the Norwegian explorer Fridtjof Nansen. For some years, Nansen had been considering an attempt to reach the North Pole with the assistance of the sheet of ice moving under the influence of the Arctic

Ocean currents from Siberia steadily towards Greenland, and passing over the Pole *en route*. Besides the strange story of the *Jeanette* wreckage, Nansen based his approach on other clues: the discovery in Greenland of an Eskimo throwing stick (used to propel a spear with extra force) of alien origin, probably Alaskan and ornamented with Chinese beads; and the fact that in the absence of native timber, Greenlanders built their boats and sledges largely of driftwood which a botanist colleague identified as Siberian in origin.

Accordingly, Nansen set out to design and construct a vessel that would allow him to undertake the same journey as this range of flotsam and jetsam. Besides specifications that would allow an expedition to live reasonably well for up to five years, Nansen put much thought into the shape and construction of the hull. Blunt-ended, immensely robust and smooth-sided, it was shaped so that when squeezed between ice floes, it would rise upwards rather than be crushed. This was the *Fram*, and in her Nansen left Norway, with a crew of twelve, in June 1893.

After initially heading round the North Cape and then eastwards along the Russian coastline, the *Fram* headed north into the ice near to the New Siberian Islands. Held fast in the ice, Nansen could then only travel where its drifting took him. The *Fram*'s construction quickly proved its worth, and soon she was riding high on top of the ice. Nansen's fore-thought also paid handsome dividends in other directions: he had fitted a windmill to power a generator, providing electric lighting once the *Fram*'s engine was unusable. The drifting was slow, and extremely tedious for the crew, though Nansen had the time to produce some superbly atmospheric paint-ings and drawings, especially of the Arctic skies and the aurora borealis.

Towards the end of 1894, the *Fram* had reached 82° 30′ N – a record at that time – but then she began to drift steadily west, rather than north and onwards towards the Pole as desired. With one of the *Fram*'s officers, Hjal-mar Johansen, Nansen decided to set off on foot for the Pole, with sledges and kayaks pulled by husky teams, in mid-March 1895. Three weeks later, with the going getting steadily more difficult and more hazardous, they passed 86°N, about 270 miles from the Pole. Temperatures sinking to minus 25°C,

and impossibly rough terrain, forced them to abandon their northward trek at this stage and head south-west for the (comparative) safety of Franz Josef Land.

The oncoming summer increased the treachery of their retreat, with patches of ice separated by leads of thaw water, sometimes fragilely bridged by fresh ice. But by early August, they had reached open water and were able to use the kayaks, lashed together catamaran-style, and sail on to Franz Josef Land. On the islands, they built a stone hut and overwintered successfully, Nansen again recording the extraordinary beauty of the clear Arctic midwinter nights, with fabulous aurora borealis displays, in delicate sketches and the most evocative prose: 'dreamland, painted in the imagination's most delicate tints'.

Towards the end of May the two men set off again in the kayaks, though not without adventures, such as having one ripped open by an angry walrus, and the drifting off (an incident so typical of Arctic exploration) of the floe to which the kayaks were moored. Nan-sen had to swim to retrieve them, and was lucky to escape with his life – a tribute to both his physical condition and to his courage after so many months of debilitating hardship. Some weeks later, camped on one of the many outlying islands of the Franz Josef group, they heard the barks of huskies, and there followed a meeting so warm yet so formally polite that it can only be equalled by the famous 'Dr Livingstone, I presume' encounter of Livingstone with Stanley in Africa.

Nansen and Johansen's rescuer was the English explorer Frederick Jackson, and the two returned with him in August to a hero's welcome in Norway. But what of the *Fram*? By strange coincidence she too returned to Nor-way that month! After more than three years, much of it spent locked fast in the drifting ice, both she and, astonishingly, all of her crew were in good shape, a tribute to their col-lective robust constitution.

Nansen himself reached only 4° away from the North Pole, and he was also in a way instrumental in its eventual conquest, as it was he who acted as President Roosevelt's adviser in nominating Robert E. Peary to spearhead American attempts to reach this cherished goal. Peary's expeditions, which began in 1886, had the single-minded aim of

RIGHT: **An unbelievable spectacle – the northern lights** *(S. Jonasson).*

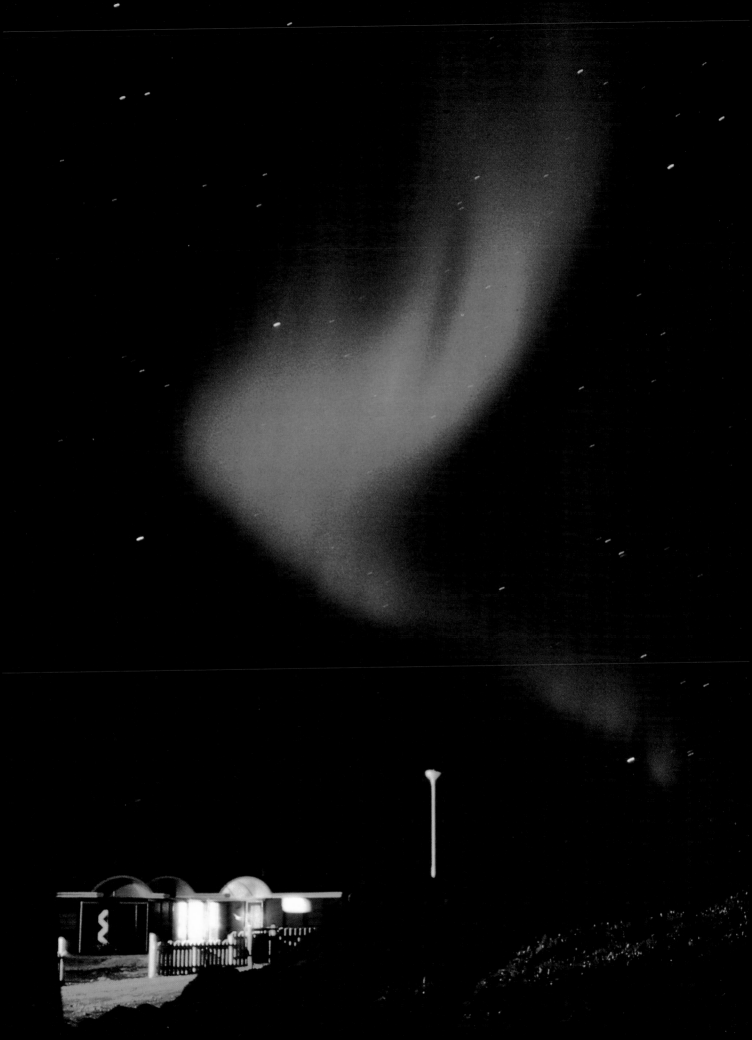

reaching the Pole: not for him the hinderances of scientific observations. His early expeditions to Greenland were the testing ground for equipment and for the men he needed to succeed in his endeavour. Peary was perhaps the first to realise the importance of selecting the right base camp, of having ample back-up supplies and personnel, but also of making the final dash with as small, fast-moving and lightly equipped a team as possible. Today the technique is familiar in assaults on major mountain peaks.

In a series of expeditions spanning twenty years, Peary found out much about the High Arctic, including the fact that Greenland was not the place to start from in a push to the Pole, but that Ellesmere Island was far better. As with Nansen, Ross and Scott, Peary's expeditions have been both brought to life and (despite the apparent contradiction) also preserved for posterity by the superb artistic abilities of one of his companions, F.W.Stokes.

Peary's persistence verges on the unbelievable. In 1905, after some twenty years of attempts and himself aged almost fifty, he made his strongest attempt to date to reach the Pole. His ship, the *Roosevelt*, like Nansen's *Fram*, was specifically designed for its task of ice-breaking a route to the north-east coast of Grant Land, carrying the supporting forces of Inuit and their dog teams. The whole expedition, though huge, aimed to dress, live and travel Eskimo-fashion, moving fast when conditions allowed, resting up in igloos when the weather was unfavourable. Sadly, the conditions were unfavourable more often than not, and they had to battle over ice ridges 30 to 50 feet high in temperatures that sank as low as 50°C below zero. Realizing that inevitably, success this time was beyond his grasp, Peary took his best dog team and established a new northernmost record of 87° 6′ before retreating and sailing back home.

In July 1908, again in the *Roosevelt*, Peary embarked on yet another attempt. Picking up some fifty Eskimos and 250 dogs *en route* in Greenland, the *Roosevelt* forced a passage during the autumn to Cape Sheridan on Ellesmere Island. By late autumn, the mass of back-up supplies on which this major expedition depended had been ferried over the ice to the 'assault' base camp at Cape Columbia. Once again, Peary was determined to use the well-proven Inuit experience of centuries in clothing his men and in travelling. He had

made the arbitrary decision to start on 1 March 1909, and described that day with the graphic facility that seems to have blessed many polar explorers: 'The stars were scintillating like diamonds... (but) the ice fields to the north... were invisible in the gray haze, which every experienced Arctic traveller knows means vicious wind... in our new and perfectly dry fur clothes... (we) could bid defiance to the wind'.

The Pole lay almost 500 miles to the north. First to depart was Captain Bartlett, with an advance party laying a chain of support facilities and food caches ahead of Peary, who also travelled with twenty-four men and nineteen sledges pulled by 133 dogs. The going was *not* easy. In Peary's own words: 'Ahead of us a dark ominous cloud upon the northern horizon, which always means open water... when the wind is blowing just right this forms a fog so dense that at times it looks as black as the smoke of a prairie fire.' Sure enough, they soon met a huge lead of open water and were forced to make camp. The lead fortunately

ABOVE: Patience and stealth – Inuit seal-hunters in the Canadian Arctic.

LEFT: Drying the cod catch, Queqertarssuq Island, Greenland.

closed overnight, but not without a terrifying crashing and grinding of the floes, which amongst other things turned the terrain into a jagged icy obstacle course, with piled-up floes (sometimes still moving) separated by awkward leads of extremely cold water. But both parties survived without loss.

As soon as their task of laying down supplies was completed, the support teams, one by one, returned to base. In mid-March they met another huge lead in the ice, one which took a week to freeze over while the expedition camped beside it. Two teams, one led by Peary himself and the other by Captain Bartlett, had deliberately taken the easiest northward journey in order to be the fittest for the final push. In the event it was Peary, with Matthew Henson and four Inuit, who set off on 2 April with five sledges and forty huskies.

Again a tribute to their endurance and physique, they managed the last 130 miles in five high-speed marches, reaching the North Pole on 6 April 1909. There they camped for two days to draw breath and plant the necessary triumphant flag (made by Peary's wife) for the photographs recording the occasion for posterity. Concentrating on their achievement, it is all too easy to minimize the decades of effort that lay behind it, and indeed the hazards of the journey back to the *Roosevelt* – but that journey too was safely and successfully accomplished, and Peary returned to an overjoyed New York.

Once the Pole had been reached, much of the intense interest in exploring the area waned, though the amazing Commander Byrd, with Floyd Bennett, became the forerunner of the now routine civil airline routes by overflying the Pole for the first time in an aircraft in 1926. Within hours yet another redoubtable polar explorer, Amundsen, (piloted by an Italian, Umberto Nobile) made the same journey in a gas-filled airship, the *Norge*. Two years later, attempting the same journey in a different dirigible, the *Italia*, Nobile crashed. He was later found alive, but sadly Amundsen, who had set off in an aircraft as part of the rescue operation, vanished without trace.

One major challenge remained, applicable only to the North Pole, located as it is on a gigantic floating sheet of ice. The first attempt to pass 'beneath' the Pole in a submarine by Sir Hubert Wilkins in 1931, commanding a vessel aptly called the *Nautilus*, failed because the vessel was damaged in a storm. It was not for another three decades that this challenge was taken up again, and then in the ultra-sophisticated (at the time) nuclear-powered submarine, delightfully also named USS *Nautilus*. On the ice surface, others from the modern generation – notably the Britons Wally Herbert and Sir Ranulph Ffynes – have emulated the prodigious journeys on foot of earlier explorers, but with the backing of late-twentieth-century technology and support systems.

On an altogether grander scale, transportation systems by air and sea have improved so dramatically in speed, efficiency, and ability, that huge quantities of raw materials, as well as smaller shipments of processed goods, are now moved routinely round the globe. Thus the pressures of traders to open up the Northwest Passage have receded. Perhaps this is just as well, bearing in mind the fickle nature of both climate and ice even in the supposedly favourable summer season, let alone amidst the savagery of Arctic winter storms. The prospect of tragedy will always be present in the Arctic, and even modern technology may be found insufficient to stem the awesome might of some of the elements.

As it is nothing more than a sheet of ice overlying the Arctic Ocean, the prospects – or indeed the risks – of future human exploitation of the mineral and other resources of the North Pole are small. These high-arctic regions are naturally much less vulnerable than the varied solid rocks of Antarctica. Possibly because of the unusual physical state of the area, there are no clear-cut treaty arrangements as to the tenure or use of the North Polar region – again a contrast to Antarctica.

In lower-arctic zones circumstances are rather different, and certainly mineral and fossil fuel exploitation is already more than a possibility in the tundra regions. The fossil fuel resources, in the form of oil, are being extracted from Alaskan fields, a process which, though paying strict (in commercial terms) regard to the fragile, slow-repairing environment of the tundra, fills many environmentalists with concern, if not dread. Certainly, were a disaster to befall the oilfield or its enormously long pipelines, it would be one on an unprecedented scale, and in a region where remedial measures would be difficult if not impossible.

RIGHT: Oilfield construction work – immense care has been taken, but the ecological hazards remain high (*Steve McCutcheon*).

3

THE SEARCH FOR THE SOUTH POLE

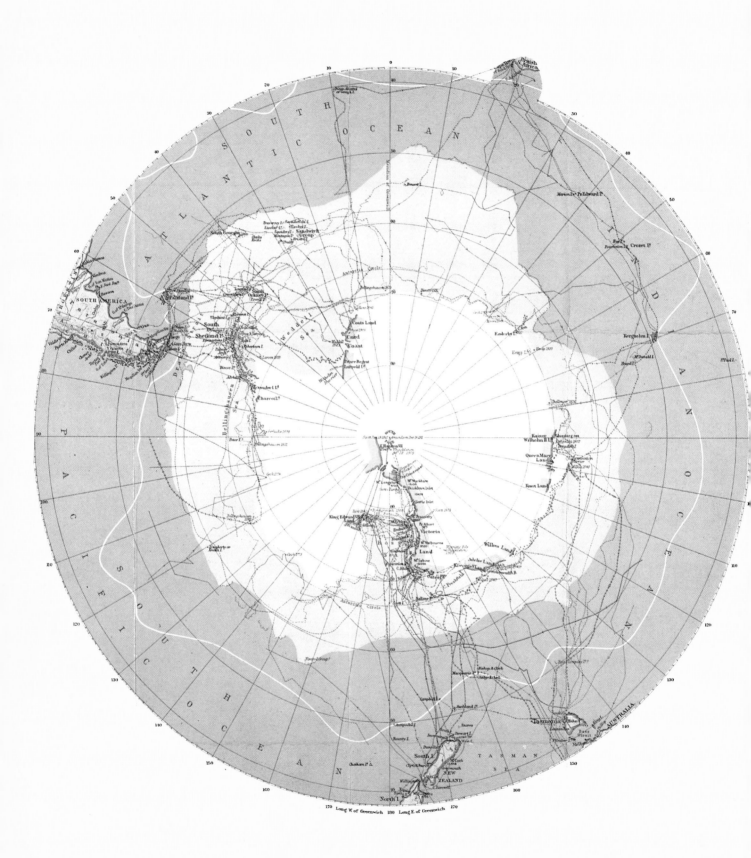

The Greek geographer and astronomer Ptolemy, writing in Egypt, then one of the centres of the civilized world, described a vast land mass far to the south. How he was aware of this land mass about 150 years after the birth of Christ remains a complete mystery, but he described it as 'Terra Australis Incognita', and depicted it as a place of evil, occupied by various legendary beasts and malign influences. This land mass, Antarctica, though now much better known, retains much of the mystery that it has always had and remains one of the most hostile, inhospitable parts on the face of the globe.

Many centuries were to elapse before a more formal exploration of Terra Australis Incognita began. During the 15th and 16th centuries Spanish and Portuguese mariners sailed south and rounded the Cape of Good Hope at the tip of Africa. Next Magellan survived ferocious seas and rounded Cape Horn, the southern tip of South America. Further to the south he saw Tierra del Fuego, and reckoned that this was the northern extremity of Terra Australis Incognita and belied its unpleasant reputation by appearing to have a reasonable climate and fertile soil. At about this time – 1555 – a map of the globe drawn by a French cartographer, Le Testu, gives a staggeringly good idea of the shape, let alone the location, of Antarctica. As with Ptolemy, how he drew this information in such excellent detail also remains a mystery.

Magellan's descriptions of this southern land, though made in error, served to fuel the spirit of adventure that was so prominent in Europe during the 18th century, particularly when potentially colonizable land was the goal. Though Antarctica has turned out to be far from hospitable and fertile, the long saga of its exploration begins in 1772, when Captain James Cook set sail from England with two tiny ships, the *Resolution* and the *Endeavour*. Cook crossed the Antarctic Circle in January 1773 – man's first knowledgeable step into this tantalizing region. Enduring considerable hardship, Cook's vessels circled the Continent over three consecutive summers, kept some distance offshore by the pack ice, returning north to revictual during the Antarctic winter months. Not surprisingly, Cook considered the area extremely cold and exceptionally risky for navigation. He predicted that no one would ever penetrate

further south than the 150 miles away from the coast that he achieved.

Early in the 19th century, sealers and whalers sailing from Britain and from the United States were to prove him wrong. Nathaniel Palmer, in the *Hero*, discovered Deception Island in the South Shetland group, and saw from the island summit the mainland of Antarctica, probably being the first person to do so. He agreed with Cook's assessment, and felt the land to be impossibly hostile, sterile and dismal, icy and mountainous, and with only small populations of fur seals. While in the southern ocean, Palmer met an expedition sent by Tsar Alexander I of Russia, commanded by Bellinghausen, who between 1819 and 1821 circumnavigated Antarctica just off the pack ice.

The first actual landing on Antarctica proper was probably made by another sealer, called John Davis, and sailing out of New Haven, Connecticut. He was convinced by the extreme height and level of snow and ice cover that the land mass on which he had set foot was actually a continent.

A year later British skipper James Weddell, with the *Jane* and the *Beaufoy*, sailed the South Orkneys, sealing, and then set off southwards, reaching 74°15′S, in the huge bay now called the Weddell Sea, well beyond Cook's record and at the time the furthest south that man had ventured. During the 1830s and 1840s whalers and sealers came to the conclusion that the operations were more practicable, and profitable, outside the Antarctic Circle than within it, and their exploratory enthusiasm dwindled. To some extent their endeavour was replaced by exploratory geographers seeking the south magnetic pole. The discovery – or rather the location – of the north magnetic pole was accomplished in 1831, and stimulated the mounting of three expeditions to find its southerly equivalent.

First away was Dumont d'Urville, despatched by King Louis Philippe for the 'glory of France'. With two ships, the *Astrolabe* and the *Zelée*, he explored much of the Weddell Sea and the northern end of the Graham Land peninsula between 1837 and 1840. On the way back from an overwintering stop in Tasmania, early in 1840 he sighted and named Adélie Land, right on the Antarctic Circle. Adélie was d'Urville's wife, and it is through her that his explorations have

PAGES 40–41: The *Lindblad Explorer*, pioneer flagship of tourism in the Antarctic, in McMurdo Sound. Scott's 1902 hut contrasts with the modern US base.

LEFT: Map of the Antarctic region *c.* 1920.

achieved almost everyday mention. Because of the height of the ice cliffs, d'Urville was unable to actually land on the Antarctic Continent, and had to make do by planting the French flag on a nearby island covered by a huge penguin colony. To these penguins also he gave the name Adélie – and by this, attractively, they are still known.

Later in January 1840, the *Astrolabe* and the *Zelée* passed almost within hailing distance of the American *Porpoise*, with Lieutenant Charles Wilkes aboard, and soon after d'Urville set course for home. Wilkes had set out from the United States in the summer of 1838, with a small fleet – the *Porpoise*, the *Peacock*, the *Flying Fish* and the *Vincennes*. Despite the number of vessels, he was really rather poorly equipped in both his ships and in the weatherproof clothing for his men, which makes his voyage from New Zealand south, then coasting along Adélie Land and covering almost one quarter of the Antarctic Circle all the more remarkable. Remarkable, too, was his brief landing on Antarctica in 1840, shortly before returning to Sydney amidst much rejoicing from his long-suffering crews.

Last to set out on the search for the southern magnetic pole was James Clark Ross, with the *Erebus* and the *Terror*. These were well built ships for use in the ice, and his men were well clad against the savage climate. They carried plentiful supplies of canned meat and canned vegetables, then a novelty but very effective in warding off scurvy. The *Erebus* and the *Terror* left the Thames in September 1839 and took almost a year to reach Tasmania, whence they departed south in November 1840. By January 1841 they had reached 74°20′, further south than anyone previously, in what is now called the Ross Sea. There Ross named the mountainous, icy and glacier-clad land he could see in the distance Victoria Land, after his reigning monarch. As d'Urville had found, landing was only possible on an offshore islet, which Ross and his second-in-command, Crozier, named Possession Island. At the end of the month, and very much to their amazement in the icy landscape, they found an active volcano which they called Mount Erebus, close to the now well-known McMurdo Sound, named after another of Ross's officers.

Ross also saw for the first time the impressive 200-foot ice-cliff – today called the Ross Ice Shelf – the visible sign of a floating mass of

ice sometimes 1,000 feet thick, stretching as far as the eye could see into the distance across the bay. In the subsequent summer, Ross returned (again from Tasmania), and by late February 1842 the two ships had penetrated south to 78°10′, a record which was to hold for several decades, before heading north, this time to the Falkland Islands. In the third summer (1843) Ross and Crozier met the Antarctic weather at its worst, a fiendish combination of gales, poor visibility due to fog or drifting snow, and perpetual hazard from drifting icebergs. They were able to push south of the Antarctic Circle only briefly, before abandoning the expedition and their hopes of locating the magnetic pole and returning home via Cape Town.

For more than the next fifty years the exploration of the world's most southerly oceans was left to the intrepid, but commercially orientated sealers and whalers, more intent on exploiting the biological richness of the surrounding seas than penetrating Antarctica's vast and barren heartland.

From the British Isles two names always to be linked with Antarctic endeavour enter the register in 1900, when Scott and Shackleton (accompanied by Wilson and Wild) landed beside Mount Erebus in McMurdo Sound to reopen the saga of Antarctic exploration proper. Between 1900 and 1904, they pushed inland some 200 miles across the Ice Shelf towards the Pole, and through the surrounding mountains a similar distance eastwards on to the main land mass.

A few more years were to elapse before

ABOVE: **Derelict whaler on Deception Island.**

TOP LEFT: **Mount Erebus from Cape Evans.**

BOTTOM LEFT: **Volcanic caldera on Deception Island in the South Shetlands.**

PAGES 46–47: **The immense Ross ice-shelf.**

'Antarctic mountain range' – painted by Dr Edward Wilson. *(Royal Geographical Society)*

the legendary race to the South Pole placed Robert Falcon Scott and Roald Amundsen, his Norwegian competitor and the first to reach the Pole, into both the history books and the annals of epic adventure.

On his earlier expedition, Scott had penetrated to within 600 miles of the Pole, and as photography (even in such harsh conditions) had developed sufficiently to provide an enthralling background to the narrative account, Scott was already famous for his exploits. Wilson's superb drawings and paintings lent additional graphic detail and amazing atmosphere to their adventures, to the wonderful scenery and wildlife, and to the perils they faced. Given fair weather, there is little, anywhere on earth, to rival iceberg scenery for spectacular and serene beauty.

Although in some ways cast in a traditionally heroic, even romantic role as an expedition leader, Scott announced in his plans to conquer the South Pole in 1909 (the year in which Peary reached the North Pole) that his team would include an unusually forward-looking and strong scientific contingent. Part of the expedition's remit was to make many scientific observations *en route*. Scott, having experienced difficulties with the huskies on an earlier expedition, elected for his polar challenge to take Manchurian ponies to haul food and other supplies at least part of the way to the Pole. Historians have inevitably been critical of this decision, but as such judgements are passed with the considerable benefits of hindsight, they may well have been overly harsh. The expedition, comparatively large and cumbersome and not fast-moving or adequately equipped to be first to the Pole if that were its only aim, left London in the *Terra Nova* in June 1910. Via New Zealand, and after considerable difficulties and delays in negotiating pack-ice off the Ross Ice Shelf, Scott set up his base at his old camp on McMurdo Sound. He set out from Cape Evans in McMurdo Sound, with Oates, Evans, Wilson and Bowers, and with ponies

that had already demonstrated their unsuitability for Antarctic blizzard conditions, on 1 November 1911.

Also goaded by the news that Peary had reached the North Pole, Roald Amundsen cancelled his plans to drift with the ice over the North Pole aboard Nansen's the *Fram*, and set out instead for Antarctica, departing almost a year after Peary's triumph was announced in September 1909. Amundsen was lucky enough to have a straightforward voyage in the *Fram*, a ship supremely well designed and adapted by Arctic experience for such a journey, and dropped anchor off the ice cliffs of the Bay of Whales. Amundsen's base was well to the east of Scott's, at the opposite corner of the ice shelf bordering the Ross Sea, but more important, also 60 miles closer to the Pole than McMurdo Sound, on terrain where every mile presents major obstacles to smooth progress – and even to survival.

Amundsen's Arctic experience was put to

good use: he and his team of four were dressed in efficient fur clothing based on that of the Inuit he had met earlier, and his four robust but lightweight sledges were pulled by dog teams familiar with the terrain and its problems and driven by experienced handlers. Thus in several ways the 'race' was an unequal one. Amundsen was single-minded in his determination to be the first man to reach the South Pole, having had the North Pole snatched from his grasp. He was very well equipped, with a totally experienced team. Scott, on the other hand, was comparatively poorly equipped, the ponies he had brought for traction quickly becoming a positive hindrance. Also, in race conditions, Scott's adherence to the meticulously planned scientific programme could not do otherwise than impede progress.

After a comparatively easy first leg across the Ross Ice Shelf, Amundsen and his team ran into severe problems in ascending to the Polar Plateau. Scott penetrated the mountain

Mount Erebus from Hut Point – painted in 1911 by Dr Edward Wilson. *(Royal Geographical Society)*

RIGHT: The crowded interior of the Cape Evans hut: remarkably well-equipped with cooking utensils.

BELOW: Scott's hut at Cape Evans.

barrier up the broad Beardmore glacier, while Amundsen was forced to make repeated attempts to bypass the numerous crevasses and ice falls on the much narrower Axel Heiberg glacier. This barrier overcome, Amundsen reached Shackleton's furthest south record (88°23') early in December,

pausing to celebrate what was already a momentous attainment. A week later the expedition reached the Pole, and celebrated in fine weather, leaving a tent flying the Norwegian flag to mark their achievement. Departing on 17 December, Amundsen's team returned to their base camp at the Bay of Whales in late January 1912, having covered almost 2,000 miles of the worst terrain in the world in just under 100 days. Such progress is a tribute to planning skills, to equipment, and to Amundsen's expertise in coping with the logistic problems of varying progress and the location of supply dumps,

plus an element of that good fortune that so often accompanies success.

Scott had appreciably less luck with the weather than Amundsen, being blizzard-bound for several days early in the trek on the Ross Ice Shelf. From then on Scott slipped steadily further behind schedule. This he had based on Shackleton's 1909 expedition, aiming to complete the round trip before the Antarctic winter made the going absolutely impossible. Just before Christmas 1911, and after Amundsen had actually reached the Pole, Scott had abandoned his ponies. In consequence, his team was nearing exhaustion having manhandled the heavy sledges up the Beardmore Glacier to the plateau. Even so, Scott was able to record cheerfully in his diary for New Year's Day 1912 that food stocks were ample and that only 170 miles of the outward journey remained. The optimism was misplaced: ferocious weather intervened, with blizzards leaving deep soft snow that made sledge hauling a superhuman effort. They of course knew nothing of Amundsen's triumph and on 18 January 1912 must have had their last vestiges of morale and sheer physical courage demolished by the sight of the abandoned Norwegian camp that signalled their arrival at the South Pole. It was at this

time that Scott wrote in his diary 'Great God! This is an awful place . . .'

The account (derived from Scott's well-kept diary that was later retrieved) of the attempted homeward journey is one of the most tragic on record. Fatigue, appalling weather,

CLOCKWISE FROM TOP LEFT: The *Terra Nova* at the ice-foot off Hut Point • The pressure ridges of the ice crack from the Barne Glacier to Inaccessible. On the left of the photograph, Captain Scott looking into Cape Royds • Grotto in a berg with the *Terra Nova* in the distance • Ponting and his telephoto apparatus • The *Terra Nova* and a berg at the ice-foot • Ponies picketed on the sea-ice • Dog team.

and frostbite dogged every step. The winter was closing in fast and blizzards were ever more frequent. Early in February the expedition, amazingly in the circumstances still intact, reached the Beardmore Glacier once again, only for the weather to become even worse. Food shortage was now added to their problems, and ill-health becomes a dominant feature in Scott's diaries. The stalwart, experienced explorer Edgar Evans died on 17 February, the heroic Captain Oates, suffering severely from frostbite, on 16 March. On 21 March they set up what was to be their last camp, only 11 miles short of their last food cache. Blizzards kept them within the tent for several days, their strength rapidly fading in the cold and with lack of food and fuel. Towards the end of the month the famous journal closes with Scott's account of the impending tragedy and of the courage of his companions. It closes with the plea: 'For God's sake, look after our people'. Eight months later, after another Antarctic winter, a relief expedition found their bodies and the diary.

Two other names, perhaps wrongly overshadowed by the powerful epic of Amundsen and Scott, should be writ large on the account of this period of Antarctic exploration: Shackleton and Mawson. Each was involved in a series of journeys. Shackleton first travelled with Scott's 1900–04 expeditions and he eventually died of a heart attack on South Georgia in 1922 as he was about to embark once again for the polar regions. Mawson's first trip was with the 1907 Shackleton expedition, and despite the rigours that he endured, he persisted with exploration until he mounted his final expedition in 1930–31.

'Endurance' could be the most appropriate epitaph for both men. Ernest Shackleton, born an Irishman but best known as the leader of the Imperial Trans-Antarctic Expedition, had as his family motto the word 'Endurance', and named one of his ships the *Endurance*. His cherished aim as expedition leader was to cross the Antarctic Continent from side to side at its narrowest point, between the Weddell Sea and the Ross Sea, via the South Pole. The *Endurance* sailed from England a few days after the declaration of the First World War, but only after an offer to join the war effort had been courteously rejected by Winston Churchill, then First Lord of the Admiralty. Reaching Antarctic seas in the New Year, 1915, the *Endurance* was immediately

in trouble. Soon she was locked irretrievably in a vast floating sea of unseasonable ice, and Shackleton and his men were forced to overwinter aboard. The *Endurance* herself was destroyed by the presence of the ice in October, and had to be abandoned. A first attempt to escape on foot to the nearest land – and possible rescue – had to be abandoned as the ice was drifting away from their goal at a greater speed than they could make over the slushy surface.

Following a four-month camp on the ice, with food supplies augmented by penguins and seals shot for the pot, Shackleton attempted again to break free from the Antarctic's grip. He and his men, in the *Endurance's* boats, headed hazardously through the gaps between floes and icebergs, making for Deception Island, a port of call for whalers. Shifting ice and a change of wind caused a change of plan, with Elephant Island – as barren as any in Antarctica – as the new target. So desolate was Elephant Island that Shackleton decided that no rescue parties would be likely to search for them there. Leaving most of his crew in camp, he set off with a handful of men for South Georgia, the nearest inhabited outpost. South Georgia lay about 900 miles away, and the seas to be crossed are still regarded as amongst the stormiest and most dangerous, with no more than the occasional brief break in their ferocity. Shackleton is recorded as sailing through waves 50 feet high and about 300 feet from crest to crest – and this in an open boat only 23 feet long with a jury-rigged canvas 'deck'. Amazingly, despite the perils of ice encrusting the rigging, shortage of fresh water and shipping seas so gigantic that the boat was filled to the gunwales, they made landfall on South Georgia only two weeks after leaving Elephant Island.

But it was on the wrong side, the south side of the island that they landed, over 150 miles away (by sea) from the sealing station that was their target. Assessing that neither boat nor men could take any further battering from the sea, Shackleton and two colleagues set out to cross the island on foot, including climbing its mountainous centre! Again risking life and limb to ice, crevasses and the cold, they set off, and after yet more incredible adventures, reached the station and organized rescue teams. So difficult were the conditions on and around South Georgia that

only at the fourth attempt, and after they had been marooned for twenty weeks and were close to starvation, was the rescue of the remainder of the crew accomplished.

Douglas Mawson, an Englishman with Antarctic experience under Shackleton and with the ascent of Mount Erebus to his credit, led the first Australian expedition to the Antarctic in 1911, exploring the comparatively novel ground of Adélie Land, unvisited since the voyages of d'Urville and Wilkes. Mawson set up his base camp in Commonwealth Bay in January 1912 at Cape Denison – a flat, featureless expanse of ice over which the winds howled with unbelievable ferocity. Mawson dubbed the camp 'the home of the blizzard', reporting gusts of up to 200 mph and how he saw a tractor weighing 1½ tons tossed into the air like a leaf. Mawson's prime purpose was to make scientific records – particularly meteorological data – and despite hardships like having to crawl on all fours to the meteorological station to avoid being blown over, his team carried out regular weather observations for ten months before setting out on a series of exploratory treks.

Mawson took with him Lieutenant Ninnis and Dr Mertz, a Swiss mountaineering and skiing expert. Covering deeply crevassed terrain, the team overcame amazing obstacles until Ninnis, his sledge, dogs and the bulk of the expedition's food vanished for ever, falling out of sight into a deep crevasse. After some hours of calling, Mawson and Mertz concluded that Ninnis must have perished in the fall, so they set off for base camp. This was some 300 miles away, and as they had food only for little more than a week, they made their best speed across the snow and ice, taking risks with further crevasses warranted only by the seriousness of their circumstances. They and their remaining dogs quickly reached a state of exhaustion and weakness, the men eventually killing the dogs in the hope that what little flesh there was left would aid their survival.

With 100 miles still to go, Mertz, severely frostbitten, died. Mawson cut the sledge in half and discarded all but his skis, ski pole, snowshoes, sleeping bag and the remnants of their food. Surviving two falls into crevasses, saved only by the rope anchoring him to his

Shackleton's hut at Cape Royds, surrounded by Adélie Penguins.

Southern Elephant Seals amongst the rusted oil vats – once the major threat to their existence – on Macquarie Island.

cross the Antarctic Continent, but steps towards the achievement of this target were slow. Aircraft reached Antarctica in 1928 when an Australian, Hubert Wilkins, flew there. A year later the South Pole was over-flown by an American, Commander Richard Byrd, and two colleagues. Apart from some difficulties in persuading their overloaded and still primitive plane to overfly the mountain fringe to the Ross Ice Shelf, they considered their journey uneventful. Although they passed through the mountains at one of the lowest points, the Liv Glacier, still they were forced to jettison food to achieve sufficient altitude!

From this time on, science played an increasing part in the Antarctic story. Byrd himself was prominent in the pre-war years and spent a four-month sojourn in isolation at a remote weather hut 120 miles inland of the coastal base Little America. A faulty stove, causing carbon monoxide poisoning, nearly cost him his life, but his poison-induced rambling radio reports alerted his colleagues at the base and a rescue party set out. Although the journey took them a month they got to the semi-conscious Byrd just in time.

After the war support logistics and technology had improved so vastly that comparatively huge expeditions could be mounted to satisfy the increasing scientific (particularly climatic, geological and biological) interest in the area. In 1946 Byrd returned in command of almost 5,000 men on a cartographic expedition, which resulted in the first chart of over 1,000 miles of coastline and in the discovery of many new islands. By the time of the International Geophysical Year (I.G.Y.) in 1957, over fifty scientific bases had been established in Antarctica by eleven nations. In the I.G.Y., Byrd was once again involved, this time in a spectacular programme centred largely on oceanography and meteorology.

The I.G.Y. show was stolen, though, by a joint British and New Zealand venture. Shackleton had set off with the Imperial Trans-Antarctic Expedition in 1915: in October 1957, forty-two years later, Dr Vivian Fuchs set out with the British Commonwealth Expedition, aiming to cross the Antarctic from the Weddell Sea to the Ross Sea via the South Pole. Simultaneously, a New Zealand party led by Sir Edmund Hillary set off to lay a train of food from McMurdo Sound towards the Pole. Even with the technological advantage of tracked,

sledge (up which he had to climb to safety as the sledge tottered on the crumbling brink of the crevasses), and enduring the 'solitary confinement' forcefully emphasized by the hardships he had to endure, Mawson made it to a cairn close to the base camp. Here food had been cached with directions to the base camp and an intermediate food depot.

Refreshed in body and encouraged in spirit, Mawson pressed on. Held up on the final stage of his journey by a blizzard, he then had to endure perhaps the most awful moment of his ordeal: he arrived at the base camp only a little later in the day than the departure of his supply ship for safe waters to overwinter. Mercifully, five volunteers had stayed in the camp in case Mawson, Mertz and Ninnis should return. Despite receiving a radio message (a novelty in Antarctic exploration) the supply ship the *Aurora* was unable to return because of bad weather, and because she was scheduled to pick up another of the exploration parties further along the Shackleton Ice Shelf. So Mawson and his men endured yet another winter, their devotion being such that yet again they maintained daily meteorological records despite the phenomenal wind speeds. Just before Christmas 1913, the *Aurora* picked them up and returned them to Australia.

Shackleton's unfulfilled ambition was to

snow-capable vehicles like Weasels and Sno-cats, the journey was terrifying for Fuchs. Crevasses abounded, and the heavy vehicles often broke through apparently robust snow bridges and got stuck. Hillary, enjoying more favourable weather and with much lighter Ferguson tractors for power, had a better journey and reached the Pole before Fuchs. There, eventually, they rendezvoused, and despite the fast oncoming winter pressed on together (after some debate) for McMurdo Sound, which they reached triumphantly on 2 March 1958, at last accomplishing the Shackleton dream.

Since the I.G.Y., scientific bases from yet more nations have flourished in Antarctica, which was nominated a 'politically and scientifically free' continent by a treaty signed in 1959 guaranteeing freedom of access for peaceful purposes. Much of the scientific work continued to be climatological, and much of the biology in the chapters that follow is based on accounts of studies mounted during the last thirty years.

A considerable amount of international interest, in the eyes of many tantamount to a major threat to this remote and largely unspoilt inhospitable continent, centres on its potential mineral wealth. Fuchs and Hillary discovered coal, and much else lies concealed beneath the ice. After six years of intermittent talks the Antarctic Treaty nations agreed in June 1988 that mineral extraction would be allowed, but subject to a strictly-applied approval process. The prospects are that Antarctica may be rich in oil and coal, copper and gold, and possibly uranium. There are however currently massive problems in mineral extraction in such a climate, but it may be that in the not too distant future, international shortages will drive engineers to overcome them. And, in much the same way as oil is now extracted from the Alaskan wilderness or from deep beneath the seabed of some of the world's stormiest oceans, valuable minerals could be brought to the surface in Antarctica.

The safeguards have been described as 'the most stringent ever negotiated': prospecting cannot even *begin* until approved by a twenty-nation panel, each with a right of veto. Both prospecting, and any eventual mineral extraction, would be subject to strict controls, and any environmental damage would be rectified by the operators, or if they were unable to comply, would become the responsibility of their sponsoring government. Not all nations are wholeheartedly in support of the convention, and international conservation opinion is united against the potential exploitation and despoliation of this cruel but magnificent wilderness.

The *Lindblad Explorer* ploughing into stormy Antarctic seas.

4

PLANT LIFE

It is difficult to conceive that anywhere else on the globe can be found challenges to the survival of plant life equal or greater than the savage conditions of the polar regions. In close proximity to the Poles themselves, the conditions normally preclude plant growth of any description, save for the occasional algal or bacterial cells that manage to survive in rare and isolated circumstances. As latitudes decrease, so a slowly ameliorating climate allows an extremely specialist flora to appear, and amazingly to flourish, often with great beauty. As with the animal life, the number of plant species is comparatively tiny compared with more temperate climate zones, but the numbers of individual plants may be colossal.

In the Northern Hemisphere, the polar ice-cap holds nothing but the chance algal cell to interest the botanist, though the seas below the ice-cap have a plant life whose story will be investigated in detail later, as it has great relevance to the marine animal life of the Arctic. By 80°N, and certainly by 70°N, appreciable areas of 'dry land' are available for colonization by plants with sufficient stamina for the task. Here, too, plants are of extreme importance. As a general rule, plants are the foundation of life: it is the photosynthetic ability of green plants (of any size, from single-celled alga to the tallest Giant Redwood) that supports the world of nature.

Through the marvellous biochemistry of the plant cell chloroplasts the sun's energy and naturally occurring atmospheric gases, aided by water and traces of minerals leached from the soil, are converted into living plant tissue. Plants themselves, abundantly varied in form and in colour, are also the basic material of all animal food chains. Terrestrial plant-eating animals – called herbivores – range in size from minute nematode worms and insects, through Lemmings, Hares and Caribou up to Elephants. Through the herbivores' dependence on plant material, various parasites (internal ones like the roundworm nematodes and tapeworms for example, or the awful warble fly, scourge of Caribou herds) derive their nourishment 'at second hand' from plants. External parasites, like the blood-sucking midges and mosquitoes so prevalent in the Arctic, benefit similarly, as do the wealth of Arctic predators particularly those dependent on the vegetarian Lemmings as a major food source, like the Ermine, Arctic Fox

and the Pomarine Skua. Though classed as carnivores or flesh eaters, even these sophisticated hunters are ultimately dependent on the plant life that sustains their prey and thus themselves.

Arctic plants are not, surprisingly, characterized by an extreme hardiness. Low growth is an obvious adaptation to keep them out of the searing cold winds, and to prevent destructive stress when covered in snow or ice, and is achieved by a compactness of growth resulting variously in tussocks, cushions, carpets or rosettes. In the stunted trees – largely Arctic Willow – branches trail low on the ground. For some shrubs like the Lapland Rhododendron, growth is staggeringly slow, and the wood therefore of extremely fine grain: a branch 25 millimetres in diameter may contain as many as 400 annual growth rings.

Microscopically, the leaves have thick, often waxy cuticles with relatively few stomata – the minute pores through which plant leaves 'breathe' or exchange gases with their environment. Such adaptations clearly help in reducing the chill factor and thus in protecting, to a degree, the plant from cold. Perhaps more important, they also cut down water loss by transpiration, which takes place largely through the stomata in the plant leaves.

This factor is important, because in essence the conditions that Arctic plants face are the same as those confronting desert plants, plus the cold. Over much of the low-Arctic, annual rainfall averages 500 millimetres or less (compared with a temperate-climate farmland average of 900–1,000 millimetres) while in the high-Arctic latitudes, annual rainfall often averages less than 100 millimetres – arid in the extreme. Having said that, in Arctic soils there is the 'permafrost' layer – lying at depths below the surface that vary with the season but are never very deep. At the permafrost layer surface the soil is perpetually frozen solid, and therefore is impenetrable both to water draining away and to roots. Thus not only must Arctic plants be resistant to cold and desiccation, but also ironically to floods and waterlogging as the warmth of the summer sunshine melts both the snow and the frozen upper soil layers.

The greater part of the landscape in the area that is here considered as Arctic is either flat or gently rolling tundra, with a vegetation perhaps best described as low

PAGES 60–61:
Arctic Buttercup.

Arctic Willow.

heath overall. The southern margins verge on willow and birch scrub, occasionally even stunted boreal conifer forest, and in the true tundra low scrub can survive in shallow ravines. There are many areas of gravelly or stony near-desert, almost devoid of vegetation, even lichens, and many areas of swamp, pools and bog which for many people give the tundra its characteristic appearance because of the flourishing and colourful mosses that surround them.

Such areas that are not tundra are rocky outcrops, or precipitous mountain ranges with peaks perpetually clad in snow or ice, or extensive ice-fields. The mountains and the major ice-caps are generally lifeless so far as plants are concerned.

The direct effects of the weather, and of snow and ice, are probably the greatest factors which influence Arctic plant growth. Second to them comes the influence of the soil itself. In the mountainous areas, and around the rock buttresses in the tundra, erosion is continuous and the fragmentation process of rocks gradually breaking down into smaller and smaller pieces creates unstable screes with little or no structure and very little organic matter: a poor habitat which few plants can master.

In the Arctic, even on the tundra, there is a second cause of soil instability, unfamiliar to the inhabitants of temperate or tropical climates and called 'solifluction'. Solifluction is caused by the alternate freezing and thawing of soil water, expanding and contracting within the soil. This process of 'frost heave' eventually produces polygonal domes of soil, sometimes 50 centimetres or more high and up to five or six metres across. They are a feature of many Arctic areas, mysterious in their regularity of design because in each polygon the soil particles are sorted so that the smallest accumulate towards the centre, while the larger stones, often arranged vertically, form a menhir-like perimeter giving every appearance of the influence of man rather than nature. Where the process of solifluction is rapid and ongoing, it produces conditions so unstable that roots cannot survive and prolonged plant growth becomes impossible.

When soils are colonized by plants, humus (the breakdown products of plant material) accumulates, leading both to greater soil fertility and stability. With increasing humus content, the soil tends to become more acidic, not only because it is insulated from the bedrock but also because snow melt-water washes out the mineral nutrients derived from that bedrock. Plants vary considerably in their tolerance of the basic or acidic nature of the soil and this is another factor determining plant distribution. Underlying rocks such as granite and sandstone contain comparatively little calcium and magnesium and produce soils that are acidic. The opposite is the case with limestone, basalts and schists, which are base-rich and produce basic (or alkaline) soils.

Many Arctic – and indeed alpine – plants tend to favour base-rich soils, but local topography has a large part to play. Snow melt water will often flow across descending levels much as spring water does. As it flows, it may flush nutrients from soils at higher levels, turning them from basic towards acidic, and as these mineral-rich leachings accumulate at the base of the 'waterfall', habitats may be created where calcium-loving plants can survive.

The plant communities that flourish on acidic soils low in basic minerals are often dominated, especially at lower latitudes, by plants like the Bilberry, Cowberry (*Vaccinium myrtillus* and *vitis-idaea*) and Bearberry (*Arctostaphylos alpinus*). Sedges and occasionally wood-rushes occur, with dwarf birches

RIGHT: **Arctic Azalea.** FAR RIGHT: **Blue Heath.** BELOW: **Bearberry.** BELOW RIGHT: **The insectivorous Long-leaved Sundew** *(Ian Rose)*.

ABOVE: Purple Saxifrage.
ABOVE RIGHT: Mountain
Avens. RIGHT: Yellow
Mountain Saxifrage.
(Ian Rose).

and willows as the 'tree' species component. This is the country of the Blue Mountain Heath (*Phyllodoce*) and the strikingly beautiful white bell-flowered *Cassiope*, frequently accompanied by *Diapensia lapponica*, tiny, cream-flowered and resembling a cross between a saxifrage and one of the Whitlow Grasses (*Draba*). Creeping Azalea (*Loiseleuria procumbens*) is an attractive addition, while the Long-leaved Sundew (*Drosera intermedia*) provides with its life-style additional fascination in lower latitudes. The sundews favour damp, deep-moss situations, and are 'insect-eating' plants. They derive various vital nutrients, including nitrogen, from the bodies of insects trapped by the sticky hairs on their leaves and slowly digested.

On base-rich soils, the 'shrubs' include the beautiful – and tasty – Arctic Bramble (*Rubus arcticus*), the Crowberry (*Empetrum nigrum*) and dwarf Arctic Willow. Three spectacularly attractive plants are frequent components of this landscape, producing stunning sheets of colour. They are the Purple Saxifrage (*Saxifraga oppositifolia*) – almost invariably present; Mountain Avens (*Dryas octopetala*) where each white flower is a joy to behold; and Moss Campion (*Silene acaulis*), forming cushions covered in white blossoms. Often dominant on gravels and screes, especially on ridges where a more stable soil has developed, is the dramatic purple-flowered Broad-leaved Willowherb (*Epilobium latifolium*). Cracks in sheltered rock faces provide a foothold for the delicate cushions of the Whitlow Grass (*Draba alpina*) – with anything *but* drab yellow flowers, and the rather similar Yellow Mountain Saxifrage (*Saxifraga aizoides*). The name saxifrage, when translated, means literally and appropriately 'rock fragmenter' as this family is paramount amongst the plants able to exploit Arctic (and alpine) environments, finding root-hold in the most hair-line of cracks.

For most Arctic plants, there is an enforced dormant season lasting while temperatures are below freezing point, though there are several, including the Glacier Crowfoot

(*Ranunculus glacialis*), that can photosynthe-size at temperatures a few degrees below zero. Once the dormant season is over, the Arctic summer is so short that plants must – and do – burst into life and flower at a phenomenal speed, as it were doing per-fectly well without the season of 'spring'. In the more open areas, the increase in the sun's warmth is a gradual one, and greatly influenced by wind chill even for prostrate or tussock-forming plants. In such circum-stances, most will take three to four weeks to come back to life and reach the flowering stage. Those plants (like the Glacier Crow-foot), which often pass the winter shrouded in a snow drift, very suddenly receive the full benefit of the sun once the snow has thawed away, and these astonishingly, may acceler-ate to flowering in a staggering six or seven days from unfreezing.

In the Arctic proper, the first flowers – including the Arctic Willow, Whitlow Grass, various chickweeds and *Potentillas*, and dramatic sheets of Purple Saxifrage – appear

Arctic Mouse-ear
Chickweed.

towards the end of May. June though is *the* month for flowers, with somewhere between 500 and 1,000 species – near the Arctic total – all in flower in some way. Purple Saxifrage is everywhere prolific, the stunted Willow 'trees' and Dwarf Birch leaf out, as do the various berry-bearing *Vacciniums*. At this time of year, frequent summer fogs may provide valuable water supplies in the form of condensation for plants in especially arid situations.

Arctic plants face (to put it in human terms) the 'difficult decision' of whether to overwinter free of snow but exposed to extreme cold and wind and the abrasive forces of blown ice crystals, or to rest protected by a layer of snow. This snow insulation can give up to 25°C of frost protection, keeping the temperature often not far below freezing; but of course this insulating blanket delays the arrival of spring warmth to restart the life-giving processes of photosynthesis. On the other hand, those plants that endured the winter in exposed situations can quickly reap the benefits of summer sunshine, but must 'beware' of bursting into leaf or flower prematurely, and being burnt-off by a sudden frost. Such a setback would not be easy to recover from in time to derive any benefit from the remainder of the all-too-short summer season.

Of the Arctic plants, many perennials hold their green leaves throughout the year, anxious to snatch any benefit from a spell of sunshine. Rather less than one per cent of the Arctic flora are annuals – in dramatic contrast to the much higher proportion of annuals in more temperate latitudes. For the annuals, what is most important is their speed in setting a prolific crop of seed, which must ripen much quicker than its southerly counterparts. To do this, and to endow that seed with sufficient nutrients to germinate and survive early seedling growth satisfactorily, makes tremendous demands on the energy turnover of the plant – demands that can be met by only a few species, hence the paucity of annuals amongst Arctic flowers.

Nor is it simply the difficulty of endowing the seed with sufficient reserves that limits annuals. The summer is so short that seeds must be set and ripen-off in one season, to germinate the next. Some plants perform this difficult task with great success, including the ubiquitous Purple Saxifrage, the Whitlow Grass and the Arctic Poppy (*Papava radicatum*). The Arctic Poppy varies in colour from cream to yellow, and its rather glossy bowl-shaped cup of petals serves as a parabolic reflector in focusing the sun's rays on to the central ovary which holds the developing ovules and later the seeds. Not only that, but the flower (as do many others) turns gradually

Arctic Poppy.

during the day like a miniature version of mankind's radio telescopes or radar dishes, always following the path of the sun and thus maximizing heat reception. Seed production may be prolific, but seedling mortality is extremely high: just to see a seedling in Arctic circumstances is a relatively rare event. Mortality results not unnaturally from sheer cold, from damp, and (perhaps surprisingly) in some circumstances from drought, the precipitation being so low.

Both annuals and perennials, if they are to set seed, have to cope with difficulties not encountered by their southerly equivalents, not least that pollinating insects are few, and erratic and unreliable in their appearance. Thus wind becomes the main pollinating agent, though many Arctic plants are self-pollinating, like Bilberry, Bearberry, and *Cassiope* and *Phyllodoce* heathers and heaths. In such circumstances vegetative reproduction (as a strawberry produces runners or a bulb small bulbils) becomes of great importance, though technically it may somewhat reduce the genetic flexibility of the plants concerned by eliminating the mixture of genes that takes place when a seed is fertilized. Many Arctic plants produce runners – the buttercups and *Potentillas* are good examples, while others produce under-

ground fleshy stolons. For some plants summer buds may in effect become bulbils when they fall off and 'germinate' or, more properly, grow.

All of these vegetative propagation strategies produce organs that are also effective for food storage, and from the plants' point of view, rather more effective storage organs than seeds. In some plants – particularly the 'viviparous' grasses like *Deschampsia alpina* and *Festuca vivipara* – the flowers are actually replaced by small plantlets that fall and grow far more effectively than could a seed in such harsh circumstances. The Alpine Bistort combines both strategies, with its upper flowers producing seeds in the normal way, and the lower ones small quick-rooting bulbils, but it seems that only rarely are seeds effectively produced at higher latitudes. *Saxifraga cernua*, a rocky ledge plant, carries a single white flower but with a series of bulbils in the leaf axils beneath it, giving it the name Bulbous Saxifrage. Those mammals and birds dependent on the Arctic vegetation for survival, especially during the harsh months of winter, exploit these sources to the full for their high nutritive values.

Autumn berries ripen from early August onwards – a further reflection of the brevity of the Arctic summer. These too are valuable food resources for a wide variety of animals, ranging (among mammals) from man to the expected Lemmings, and the perhaps less-expected Arctic Foxes and Brown Bears. Among birds too there are unusual beneficiaries as the various Arctic gull species and even the extremely predatory Pomarine Skuas vie with Ptarmigan and Lapland and Snow Buntings. The berry supply is as colourful as it is varied, ranging from clusters of bright red Cranberries and delicious Cloudberries (raspberry-like except for their yellow colour) to spherical midnight-blue Bilberries, borne singly and often sparingly on Azalea-like shrubs, and inky-black Crowberries on heather-like plants.

The landscape is not uniform, nor indeed is its flora. A number of factors may produce localized conditions that may dramatically affect flowering plants. The problems, and benefits, of late-lying snow cover have already been explored so far as the plant is concerned, but the visual impact on the scenery is also distinctive. As the snow patch gradually thaws, so the covered plants burst into life: in many circumstances this leads to the plants growing and flowering in roughly concentric bands depending on the depth of the snow or the time at which it thawed. Increased altitude obviously delays snow thaw, as may deep gullies or unfavourable slopes. Occasionally snow beds may lie unbroken for many years without a thaw: amazingly, the Glacier Crowfoot, the woodrush *Luzula*, and the Arctic Willow have the ability to survive such continued hardship, and to emerge and grow should a thaw eventually occur.

Around seabird colonies, be they on the flat or on cliffs or crags, the high nitrogen levels resulting from copious supplies of the birds' droppings near the nest result in a comparatively lush growth of those plants favouring nitrate-rich locations. Sorrel and various dandelions and chickweeds are encouraged by such conditions to form dark green hummocks, often surrounding a nest site that has been used year after year. On rocky nesting areas, the seabird guano induces the growth of characteristic orange lichens, so conspicuous as to make nesting cliffs visible and identifiable as such from miles away.

But what are these lichens? It is said of them that they inhabit some of the most forbidding regions of the earth, occurring further north – and further south – than any other plant, and elsewhere at altitudes exceeding 6,000 metres. Lichens are often described as 'lowly' plants, but on closer inspection they are very sophisticated – and indeed are still very imperfectly understood. On rocks they are perhaps typically roughly circular encrustations of very dry and papery material, often greenish or greyish in colour but occasionally bright yellows and oranges. These are the 'crustose' lichens, and are characterized by extraordinarily slow growth: in the Arctic, the estimated age of some specimens exceeds 4,000 years, with a growth-rate rarely reaching one millimetre in a year.

Lichens are clearly not only robust but adaptable: polar regions, deserts, even the backs of slow-moving insects are all recorded habitats. One even survives – and grows – submerged in freezing waters in the Antarctic. They are, however, sensitive to industrial pollutions, and are today often used as indicator plants to demonstrate the presence of harmful levels of toxic gases in the atmosphere.

A lichen is a botanical cooperative, a mutually beneficial partnership between an alga on the one hand and a fungus on the other. Almost always it is just one algal species and one fungus that form this association, a symbiotic relationship called mutualism. Almost always, too, each partner is capable of survival on its own, but not necessarily so successfully or adaptively. The alga is often a single-celled one, either from the blue-green group or from the green group. The fungus is usually an Ascomycete (which group hold their spores in a small sac called an ascus). A typical lichen has a lower surface largely composed of strands of the fungal partner, called hyphae, with very occasional algal cells. Above this is a thicker layer (though often still measured in fractions of a millimetre) where the hyphae are less closely packed, and then the surface layer, again of fungal hyphae (often with fruiting bodies of the fungus) with the occasional embedded algal cells.

A cooperative that can continue for 4,000 years is obviously a stable one: what benefits do the partners derive from this mutualism? Fungi lack chlorophyll, and are thus incapable of photosynthesis: they normally derive their energy for growth at second hand, for example from decaying plant material or as parasites on living material. In a lichen, the algal cell can manufacture its food by photosynthesis, converting carbon dioxide and water into carbohydrates using the energy of sunlight and the synergistic capability of the chloroplasts to achieve this. Excess carbohydrate is excreted by the alga, and very swiftly (within minutes) is taken up by the fungal partner and converted into further carbohydrates that the fungus can use for its own nutrition. Possibly also the alga provides some vitamins and trace elements necessary for good growth. In exchange, the alga receives shelter – many of the algae involved in lichens have a dislike of strong sunlight, and thus on their own do not maximize their photosynthetic potential, so this may be a reasonably important factor. The fungus, too, is adept at taking moisture from misty atmospheres, and this water becomes readily available to the alga.

Though fascinating in themselves, many lichens form part of the complex web of animal and plant life in the Arctic, but one, called 'reindeer moss' plays a more striking part. Grey-green and much branched, reindeer moss (*Cladonis rangifera*) most resembles the antlers of a Reindeer (or Caribou) in miniature, fronds rarely exceeding two or three centimetres in length. Caribou and Musk Oxen rely heavily on reindeer moss as their staple grazing diet through the long months of winter when green plant food is to all intents and purposes unavailable. The lichens are highly nutritious, being comparatively rich in carbohydrate for their volume, and are thus an effective food for winter when energy demands are at their highest in the extreme conditions. They are, though, low in protein and would not make a year-round balanced diet. Also, in areas where there has been exposure to various forms of radiation – for example nuclear weapon test areas, or after a major nuclear power station disaster, radioactive strontium and caesium can be absorbed in quantities sufficient to be dangerous to the Caribou.

Elsewhere lichens have a long history as the basis of primitive but effective dyes, and the chemical indicator litmus, known to every schoolchild, is derived from a species of *Roccella* lichen. Medicines, too, have long been derived from lichens in Iceland, and it would seem that current research will reveal more antibiotic and other curative properties.

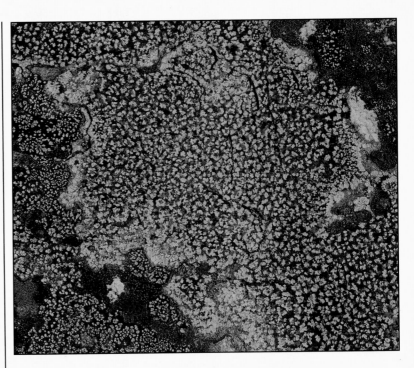

Rhizocarpon lichen.

With their excessively slow rate of growth, the widespread, ground-covering lichen species like reindeer moss can very readily be destroyed by modern motorized Arctic vehicles, particularly those with four-wheel drive or caterpillar tracks. In moments, plants like the lichens (or the similarly slow-growing Lapland Rhododendron) can be destroyed, and may take not just decades or centuries, but millenia to replace. There is an evident paradox here in the speed with which some other Arctic plants rush into bloom once the snow has thawed, but the paradox is more apparent than real for two reasons. One is that the rapid blossoming is dependent on a root system that may have taken many years to establish, so that though the flower is ephemeral, the plant is aged. The other is that should that flower – and plant – be destroyed, then a new seedling has to survive the battle with the elements to replace it, and the odds are stacked heavily against its survival. This is indeed a fragile environment, and one at great risk at times when exploration, particularly seeking new fossil energy sources, is running at fever-pitch.

Plant growth in the sea in polar regions is of extreme importance. Sea temperatures are inevitably higher than those on land when the latter fall well below zero, so in effect the sea offers a comparatively sheltered environment. Despite this, during the winter months when protection from the savage land environment would be most beneficial, there is insufficient light (let alone sunshine!) for the process of photosynthesis, so plant growth below the waves also ceases.

In polar regions the typical algae of temperate coasts - the popular 'seaweeds' – also have their representatives, but towards the Poles, as in warmer climates, they do not feature largely in any major food chains. Fish (to a small extent) and molluscs (to a larger one) may browse on seaweed fronds, but few indeed are dependent on these large algae for much more than shelter or concealment.

Of much greater importance are the minute algae – often single-celled and microscopic in size – that constitute the phyto- (or plant) plankton. The numbers of these tiny plants vary hugely with the season, and with the sea conditions, as they tend to sink deeper to more settled water when the seas are rough. In both polar regions they are always present, but numbers are low during the winter months when much of the phytoplankton is to be found on the sea floor in the form of highly resilient spores or cysts with a robust protective cell wall. Phytoplankton, like higher plants, need a sufficiency of light for photo-

synthesis, the process on which all green plants depend. This is absent during the dark days of autumn and winter, and it is not until May in the Northern Hemisphere, November in the Southern, that this marine plant life begins to flourish.

Over the long winter months, plenty of nitrates, phosphates and other necessary chemicals accumulate in the seabed ooze and in the sea itself, more than sufficient to fuel a speedy, even explosive upsurge in growth late in the polar spring when light levels become adequate for photosynthesis. This 'bloom' of the phytoplankton may last anything from one to three months, depending on conditions. Particularly influential are upwellings of cold water from the depths, which bring with them to the plankton floating near the surface fresh supplies of these vital nutrients – almost fertilizers. Such upwellings may be local – at the face of reefs or a grounded iceberg, for example, or on a grand scale at the confluence of major ocean currents.

The simple plants of the phytoplankton are food, particularly for the minute animals of the sea, the zooplankton, which range in size from single-celled creatures not much larger than the phytoplankton to larval crabs, sea-urchins and sea-slugs and the krill which form the staple diet of crab-eating Seals, Adélie Penguins and the baleen or whalebone whales of both polar regions. On the zooplankton feed a range of creatures, including fish and birds, and on these yet other carnivores, the polar predators, depend. Southern polar ocean krill, more properly the Antarctic Krill (*Euphausia superba*) has been described as the most abundant animal on earth. It is a shrimp, around 65 millimetres long, which gathers quantities of phytoplankton with its feather-like fore-limbs, shovelling them into an ever-active digestive system.

If there is a considerable degree of uniformity (apart from the calendar months in which they flourish) in the sorts of marine plants and animals that form the phytoplankton and the zooplankton in both polar regions, the same cannot be said of the higher plants. Comparatively speaking, poor though its flora may be in comparison with both temperate or tropical landscapes, the Arctic is rich indeed compared with the Antarctic. There are, of course, striking differences in the areas adjacent to the two Poles: in the south, the

Massive beds of kelp are as much a feature of polar shores as of temperate ones.

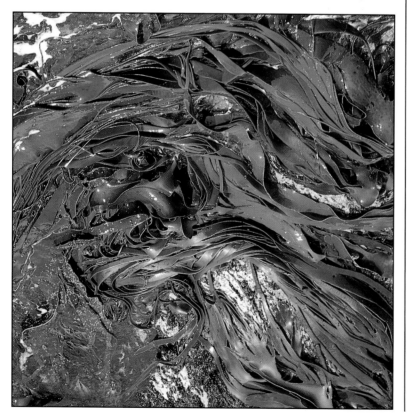

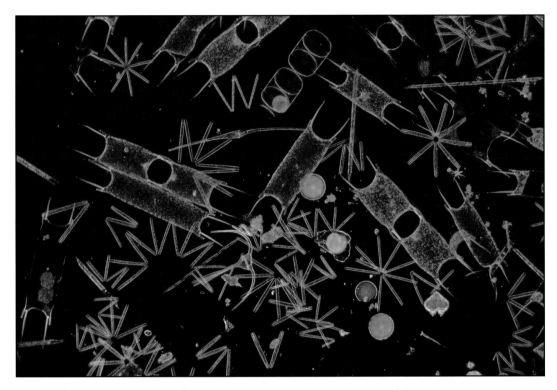

The variety of microscopic phytoplankton is as amazing as their structures are beautiful, especially the diatoms that predominate here (D. P. Wilson).

immediate polar region is solid rock, largely capped in ice of great thickness; in the north, it is a drifting sheet of ice of great area but relatively little depth, often only a few metres thick. But both these areas are so savage climatically that terrestrial plant life can only extremely rarely survive: the major differences, perhaps surprisingly, lie in those parts of the polar regions distant from the Poles themselves. Here again, striking differences are engendered by the contrasting physical geography of the two areas.

The north polar region is a polar sea, encircled almost entirely by major land masses, stretching away and expanding into temperate and then tropical climates. A glance at the globe will show that although the Antarctic Continent is itself a very considerable land mass, it is ringed by oceans. In the north, both northern Greenland and Ellesmere Island lie well within 10° of latitude of the Pole, and within the Arctic Circle (at 33.3° latitude south of the Pole) there are massive amounts of tundra and other landscapes embracing northern Scandinavia, European and Asiatic Russia, Arctic Canada and Alaska, and numerous major island groups such as Novaya Zemlya and Spitzbergen.

In the south little other than the chill bulk of the Antarctic Continent lies within the Antarctic Circle, 33.3° of latitude north of the Pole. North of this lies a circumpolar belt of ocean almost 20° of latitude wide, penetrated only by the finger-like Antarctic Peninsula of Grahamland stretching towards Tierra del Fuego, the southernmost tip of South America, lying at about 55°S. Within this oceanic belt lie only a handful of remote and comparatively small island groups. South Georgia, South Sandwich, South Orkney, South Shetland, and, slightly further to the north, the Falkland Islands lie roughly south to south-east of South America. Some considerable distance away (90° of longitude) lie Marion and Prince Edward Islands and the Iles Crozet, and even further (about 110°) Mount Ross and Heard and Macdonald Islands, with (at 210°) Macquarie Island lying south of Australasia. And that is roughly the sum total of land south of 50° S in the Southern Hemisphere. The southern tip of New Zealand lies at about 50° S, of South Africa at 40° S: the preponderance of ocean is overwhelming. Thus the flora of the southern polar region is constrained greatly by the impossible climate of the Antarctic Continent itself, and by the lack of land masses and extreme isolation and inhospitability of such few small island groups as do exist.

On the Antarctic Continent itself, only two vascular (or higher) plants have been found,

both cushion-forming like many Arctic plants, and both on the Antarctic Peninsula to as far south as 68°. One is the grass *Deschampsia antarctica*, the other a pearlwort, *Colobanthus quitensis*. Beyond this the flora is heavily dominated by mosses, liverworts and lichens, with eighty-odd, twenty-five and about 150 species respectively. Many of these comparatively simple plants aggregate in what almost amount to colonies. By gathering in mats and cushions they gain extra protection from the elements, and probably improve their ability to collect water, and indeed reduce water-loss by transpiration. The Antarctic land mass amounts to some 14 million square kilometres, of which around two per cent is free of ice as rocky crags or stony desert. In such circumstances, it is not too surprising that the lichens penetrate furthest south, with a record at 86°, and that at an altitude of almost 2,000 metres, only about 400 kilometres from the South Pole.

The survival strategies evolved by these Antarctic plants closely parallel those in the northern polar regions: the lichens tend to be dark-coloured, thus absorbing such sun-warmth as there is to maximum effect; all are low growing, avoiding wind damage and, even more important, dessication. As the temperature falls towards winter, so the water content of their cell-sap is reduced, allowing chemicals, particularly salts and sugars, to accumulate in quantities appreciably higher than normal which function effectively as 'antifreeze' agents. This prevents the formation within the plant cells of ice crystals which would be mechanically very destructive, even of the cell walls.

Some Antarctic lichens can manage to 'tick-over' at temperatures as low as −20°C in the open, while one alga – a relatively simple blue-green one – has evolved a new life-style by living within the shelter of thin cracks in rocks: an astonishing but obviously effective adaptation for a green plant dependent on light for survival. Similarly extraordinary is the minute single-celled alga *Pyramimonas gelidicola*, which looks like a miniature jelly fish and propels itself through the water by lashing a tiny whip-like flagella. The ice-free coastal strip of Antarctica contains a number of lakes, much saltier than the sea (often ten times the salt concentration) and thus resisting freezing until temperatures fall below −20°C or thereabouts. *Pyramimonas* cell con-

tents are rich in polyols (complex organic molecules) and in sugar-derived alcohols, both of which protect the cell as 'anti-freeze'.

Other algae have evolved to survive in snow drifts, including one that produces a copious pink 'stain' to the snow, or to tolerate – and even benefit from – the excessively high concentration of nitrates produced by the guano surrounding penguin rookeries. Others survive in gravel or sand, and some even in the shelter under rocks, but interestingly it is often beneath light-coloured or translucent quartz that such algae flourish. Fungi, too, have been found in the Antarctic, with a few mushroom-like forms occurring towards the tip of the Antarctic Peninsula and on some of the island groups.

The vegetation of these island groups scattered around the Antarctic land mass is as much as anything restricted by their extreme isolation, both one from another and from the nearest temperate major land masses. Though in human terms their climate would be considered quite harsh, compared with the Antarctic land mass itself it seems quite benign. This serves to underline the restrictions on plant life imposed by the isolation, for otherwise far more plants would flourish than actually do.

South Georgia, lying between 54° and 55°S, is one of the most mountainous of Antarctic islands, rising as a snow-clad ridge abruptly and apparently directly out of the ocean. The ridge of mountains reaches almost 3,000

The lichen *Caloplaca regalis* on King George Island.

LEFT: Once the slightly more temperate latitude of the Falkland Islands is reached, plant life becomes more diverse.

Tussock Grass dominates the vegetation of most sub-Antarctic islands.

Where, in more exposed areas, other vegetation becomes established, it is the typical Antarctic flora of mosses and lichens that holds sway. There are patches of higher plants: two species of Burnet, for example, one of them *Acaena ascendens* peculiar to South Georgia. Also present are the bedstraw *Galium antarcticum* and the delicately miniature Antarctic Buttercup (*Ranunculus biternatus*) only a couple of centimetres high. In sheltered low-altitude rocky gullies there are four species of fern: one of them, the Brittle Fern (*Cystopteris fragilis*) with the most astonishing of world distributions, as it is found elsewhere in Chile, on Spitzbergen in the Arctic and in Ethiopia!

Choosing a more southerly example, the South Shetlands archipelago lies between 62° and 63° S. Here the average annual temperature has fallen to −3°C, with a range from −30°C to +15°C. Rainfall is frequent and often heavy, with a great deal of cloud in consequence. As 'summer' days are often fog-shrouded, there is little sunshine, and snow or frost can occur at any time during the year. The South Shetlands vegetation is closely similar to that of the Antarctic Peninsula, dominated by mosses and lichens which are often very spectacular near penguin rookeries or seal colonies. Two vascular plants occur, the two Antarctic stalwarts: the hairgrass *Deschampsia antarctica* and the pearlwort *Colobanthus quitensis*.

metres at its highest point. South Georgia serves as an example of the milder climatic conditions: the average temperature over the year is about 2°C, with a minimum of around −15°C and a maximum of about 20°C. Lying as it does in the 'roaring forties', wind (often gale-force) is a predominant feature. Overall the picture is windy, cloudy, wet and cold, with frequent fogs in summer and rain or snow on average on perhaps 200 days each year.

Much of the island is perpetually clad in snow or ice, especially the higher altitudes. Elsewhere there are extensive screes and boulder fields, but where there is vegetation, it is the Tussock Grass (*Poa flabellata*) that dominates the scene visually as well as botanically. This coarse, fast-growing grass is often waist-high, and its tussock structure and overlapping leaves usually exclude other plants.

Thus, though those regions in close proximity to the two Poles may show a certain similarity in that the sheer hostility of the terrestrial environment more or less precludes plant growth, the regions that are described as the Antarctic and the Arctic for the purposes of this comparative survey differ dramatically in their plant life. The Arctic, ringed by land (much of it tundra) is far richer in its flora than the Antarctic. The physical geography of the latter – largely hostile ocean with island groups few and very far between, and with the major land masses containing potential colonists set at a great distance – produces such isolation that the flora can only be described as impoverished, though often it is marvellously fascinating in its adaptations for survival in the harshest terrain on earth.

Such a concept of the impact of remoteness

and climate on the flora is strengthened by a brief investigation of the Falkland Islands, lying rather further to the north at about 51° S and perhaps only marginally describable as Sub-Antarctic islands. On the Falklands both the better climate (with the larger, more complexly-organized human population that it encourages) and the proximity (about 500 kilometres away to the west) of mainland South America are readily apparent. The influence of the Falkland Islanders them-selves – and their farming – is evident in the number of introduced plant species. These alien plants – about eighty-seven out of a total of some 260 species – exceed in number the endemic species, those native to (and restricted to) the Falklands, which amount to only a dozen or so species.

The increase in plant life is not only reflected in the much larger number of spe-cies, but also in the number of plant families represented. Thus there are a dozen club-moss and fern families, each with two or three species. At the other end of the scale there are half a dozen rushes in the Juncaceae and seventeen sedges in the Cyperaceae, and over forty grasses, interestingly more than half of them are introduced species and none of them endemic.

In addition there are forty-two other flower-ing plant families, mostly with only a few representative species and mostly well known from temperate climates. These include the nettles, docks, chickweeds, but-tercups, crucifers (the cabbage family), saxi-frages (with *Saxifraga magellanica* the only species, in contrast to the richness of this family in the Arctic), roses, vetches (the pea family), cranesbills, heathers, violets, daisies, umbellifers (the carrot family), and even four species of orchids. Daisies, the *Compositae*, top the list with thirty-six species, of which eight are endemic, including the delicate white Vanilla Daisy (*Leuceria suavedens*) which smells powerfully of chocolate. Other well-represented families are the buttercups (*Ranunculaceae*) and chickweeds (*Caryo-phyllaceae*) both with eleven species and the vetches (*Leguminosae*) with nine. All of this is in striking contrast to the floral poverty of those sub-Antarctic and Antarctic island archipelagos only a few degrees further south.

The introduced plants give an immediate 'homely' feel to the visitor to the Falklands,

including as they do Hart's Tongue Fern, Mouse-ear Chickweed, Curled Dock and Corn Cockle, now ironically often faced with extinction in the Northern Hemisphere because of the dramatic efficiency of modern herbicides in cereal crops. Others include Annual Nettle, Shepherd's Purse, Yellow Stonecrop and Gorse, now picturesquely abundant and clearly flourishing in maritime conditions closely akin to those of its northern native habitats. White Clover, Red Dead-nettle, the Lawn Daisy, Groundsel and Creep-ing Thistle are also on the list and give a clear indication of the northern temperate farmland origin of most of these plants, many of which would be familiar and normally be called 'weeds' by a European farmer or indeed gardener.

Gardeners, though, would also recognize some of the genuinely native plants because they occur commonly in cultivation, normally to be seen on nursery lists or in garden centre displays. These include the ornamental berry-bearing *Pernettya pumila*, called the Mountain Berry by the islanders, and the miniature pink *Oxalis enneaphylla*, the dwarf iris *Sisirhynchium chilense*, and the beautiful yellow Ladies Slipper *Calceolaria fothergillii*, which now grace many European rockeries.

The delightful Falkland endemic, Lady's Slipper.

5
INSECTS

Compared with more temperate latitudes, Arctic insects, though numerous, represent a pathetically small number of species: a simple reflection of the fact that only a tiny fraction of the world's insects have evolved the ability to survive in the Arctic ecosystem. In all, there may be only a few thousand species – compared with a 'world-total' of two million beetle species alone. The two-winged flies – Diptera – predominate, including the typical flies, and gnats, mosquitoes and midges. They form, in most Arctic areas, somewhere between 60 and 70 per cent of the species and a far greater proportion than this of the total insect bulk, or biomass. This contrasts with the rating of the Diptera in temperate latitudes, which normally lies between 10 and 20 per cent of the species to be found.

Others include the aquatic Caddis Flies, a range of beetles and bugs of many sorts. Amongst the bugs – Hymenoptera - bees, wasps and the parasitic ichneumonids are reasonably widespread. There is a rather surprising presence of butterflies and moths – seemingly so fragile and so much a part of warm or even tropical ecology – but again the number of species is minute compared with the tropics. Some groups familiar in temperate climates are notably absent: dragonflies, lacewings, grasshoppers and crickets, for example, are extremely scarce on the southern fringes of the Arctic, or absent altogether.

In discussing the true insects, and how they survive in Arctic circumstances, it is practical to include other small animals – those which are without an internal bony skeleton and are gathered into the immense phylum of the invertebrates. In the Arctic most of these live within the soil or on its surface, and they include the spiders, mites, centipedes and so on, with jointed legs, and the nematode worms. All have to endure the same rigours, and all share with the insects the physiological and behavioural adaptations that allow them to do this. In many cases, for these invertebrate animals, the 'winter' lasts for nine months of the year. It is tempting to assume that this must represent a period of extreme hardship, which in a sense it does, but paradoxically, during those nine months many of the problems of life have been removed: no predators are able to seek them out, and they need not themselves hunt for food.

What is imperative is an ability to withstand freezing and to conserve food reserves while doing so. Most invertebrates, insects included, seem to overwinter as larvae: eggs are unusual, and rather surprisingly, to overwinter as pupa, safe in the protection of some form of cocoon, is the exception rather than the rule as might be expected. All are able to lay down considerable stores of fat, and many seem able to adjust the fluid content of their cells so that ice crystals are avoided. The latter are potentially very damaging as they form, in much the same physical way as they disrupt by expansion, pipes in frozen-up domestic plumbing systems. Most invertebrates overwinter in the soil, which gives a surprising degree of protection: at the harshest times of midwinter, at 10–15 centimetres down in the soil there may be only a few degrees centigrade of frost, when air temperatures above may be 30 or 40°C below zero.

The tundra pools also freeze solid, and the invertebrates in that water or in the mud at the bottom freeze solid too, and rest in suspended animation until the spring. In deeper lakes, some water may remain unfrozen, and in this the larval invertebrates congregate, to all intents and purposes inert to conserve their precious supplies of stored energy.

Some larval stages – notably those of the butterflies and moths – though able to withstand the freezing would be immensely vulnerable to the damp, possibly waterlogged conditions as the thaw starts and melt water begins to flow. Amazingly, at the end of the summer the caterpillars spin protective cocoons or webs above ground, often in the stunted vegetation, and somehow manage to exist in the frozen state until they thaw out in the comparative warmth of spring.

Although spring – or summer – may start in May, insect life is still sparse: too sparse to support small purely insectivorous birds, and too sparse, or perhaps too difficult of access in the soil which is still largely frozen, to feed the vast numbers of breeding wading birds beginning to arrive from the south. These birds must arrive on their breeding grounds with an adequacy of food reserves, in the form of body fat, to tide them over until the thaw is properly under way. On warm days the occasional fly will make an appearance, and the terrestrial predators, like spiders and the velvety red trombiculid mites, will be active. Within their protective webbing, overwinter-

PAGES 78–79: **Overnight dew on a sub-Arctic** *Sympetrum* **dragonfly, still waiting for sufficient warmth from the sun to resume its daily life.** *(Larry West).*

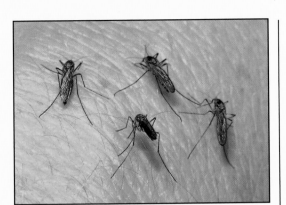

Aedes mosquitoes, one of several insect scourges of warm-blooded animals in the Arctic *(Larry West)*.

ing caterpillars will twitch, anxious to feed and complete their life cycle.

During June, but naturally normally earlier in the lower latitudes of the Arctic, the first bumble bees and butterflies appear on the wing. The first mosquitoes also appear then, a prelude to the hordes to come later in the year. By mid-June, on any warm day the soil surface may be a hive of activity among spider, mite and Springtail (Collembola) communities. Butterfly and moth caterpillars can be found, Arctic Fritillaries and Sulphurs, and the 'woolly bear' larva of the Redtail Moth, with many of the superficially nondescript smaller moths, the Microlepidoptera. Even at these high latitudes, with all the irregularity in distribution, numbers and timing of caterpillars, parasitism is established as an effective way of life for some insects. The occasional unusually motionless caterpillar will, on dissection, prove to contain the larva or pupa of a parasitic hymenopterid ichneumon, steadily eating its host alive from within. Other caterpillars may be attacked by numbers of larvae of parasitic flies.

At this time of year, a host as large even as a Caribou may have problems with parasitic insects. The previous summer, Warble Flies may have laid eggs on the fur on the backs of a reasonable proportion of the Caribou in any one herd. These quickly hatch and burrow into the Caribous' skin, and, while still tiny, maggots migrate round the body tissues until the autumn when they come to rest under the skin of the back, usually near the backbone. Here they continue to grow through the winter and spring in a blood- and pus-filled cavity, breathing through a small air-hole gnawed in the skin. The larval parasite emerges full-grown in June – this understandably causing great irritation to the Caribou. In any individual, parasitic numbers are usually small, but occasionally a weak Caribou may be almost eaten alive by hundreds of Warble Flies, and it is such individuals that fall easy prey to hunting Wolves.

The emerging maggot drops to the ground and immediately pupates, to emerge as the full-grown fly later in the summer. The adult does not eat: it emerges from the pupa with an adequate fat store and with the single duty of mating, and for the female laying eggs. Caribou seem to be well aware of the hazards of Warble Flies, and will do all in their power to avoid a fly seeking to lay its eggs, but escape is difficult. Interestingly, a piece of evolutionary common sense protects the Caribou calves, which the Warble Flies do not attack, no matter how defenceless they may seem. Such an attack on a calf could easily prove fatal to the animal, and a well-balanced relationship between a parasite and its host demands that the host is not killed, for if this were to be the case the parasite would die too, literally having eaten itself out of house and home.

During June, when the air is still, various other flies are on the wing, buzzing around bluebottle-like. The larvae of many of these will have developed in seething hordes on the freshly-thawed rotting carcases of winter casualties, particularly among the Caribou. At the end of June Craneflies – popularly called 'daddy-long-legs', but more properly Tipulid flies – emerge from damp soils where their plump larvae have over-wintered. As the ground thaws, so they move upwards to pupate just below the surface. Slim male and broad-bodied females emerge for their very short, free-flying, non-feeding lives. Once mated, the female quickly deposits her eggs for the life cycle to resume. By mid-June, having fed voraciously since they started moving after the winter freeze, butterfly and moth caterpillars have pupated. Some merely turn leathery, while others spin a silken cocoon attached to a sheltered stem or the underside of a leaf.

June and July, as the warmest times of the year, naturally see most insect (and other invertebrate animal) activity. Lakes, pools and boggy soil teem with the larval insect life so important to the breeding wading birds and wildfowl. Besides mosquitoes, gnats and midge larvae, tiny Water Fleas or *Daphnia* are also prodigiously prolific, feeding fish like the Arctic Char. On still days, myriads of

Shipwrecked vessels (this the *'Lady Elizabeth'* in Stanley Harbour on the Falklands) are a major source of accidental introductions of both animals and plants.

midges and mosquitoes can appear as if by magic. They have very sensitive infra-red heat detector capability, and can sense a warm-blooded man or beast at an astonishing distance, the smoke-like dancing columns of flying insects relentlessly homing-in on their target. Eventually the victim is smothered in an infuriating and extremely uncomfortable cloak of insect life. Hated Blackflies produce an audible buzzing as they advance, and were described by one Arctic explorer as the 'most ferocious things in the Arctic'. They seem able to penetrate even the most dense and complex layers of feathery plumage, fur or clothing in their search for exposed skin: not just the soft parts, but also hard skin near beaks and feet. In this they plunge their minute, needle-sharp mouthparts to suck out the blood meal vital to the successful completion of their life cycle. As they stab in their mouthparts, so they release an anti-coagulant so that the blood does not clot, and it is this that triggers the allergic reaction in the skin and consequent swelling and intolerable itching.

By mid-August, insect life in the open air has become difficult to sustain. Gone are the hordes of midges, Blackflies and mosquitoes, with the adults all dead having laid eggs long ago, so that the larvae are reasonably safe to overwinter in the soil, or in pond water.

Terrestrial arthropods like spiders and mites seek shelter in the soil or in the litter of decaying lichens and vegetation. Surprisingly, perhaps, most Arctic insects go through the full series of life-cycle stages: egg, several larval stages, pupa and adult. Evolution does not seem to have found short cuts to this process, which will be extended over two seasons rather than truncated in any way. Not only must they be able to survive the winter cold (usually as a larva, occasionally as a pupa, rarely as an egg or adult) but their life cycle must be geared not just to the brevity of the Arctic summer but also to the abrupt transitions from winter to summer and summer back to winter.

Though conditions may be extremely harsh in winter in the Arctic, a reasonable range of invertebrate life has adapted to the circumstances and is able to survive, even in some cases (particularly the Blackflies, midges and mosquitoes) to flourish in that season. The contrast is striking in the Antarctic, particularly in the scarcity of insect life, where over most of the region only two tiny species of midge represent this gigantic assemblage of animals.

As in the Arctic there are several invertebrate groups represented, almost entirely confined to the soil, plant litter or water. More than 100 such species come from the soil mites, the Collembola (or springtails), some Tardigrades (which look under the microscope like tiny, transparent, rotund six-legged bears) and Rotifers (interestingly most of them endemic species), and at least fifty recorded species of Nematode worms. Doubtless more remain to be discovered, particularly on the sub-Antarctic islands, but their number is unlikely to be great. Most of these proceed through a series of larval stages, with intervening moults, before they reach adulthood. In consequence, despite their microscopic size, these larval stages may take more than a year to complete – not least because around nine months of that year are spent locked in some form of frozen inertia.

The protection afforded by the soil, or by water (no matter how salt), is clearly of great importance. Soil-dwelling imposes practical limitations on size, and almost all of the Antarctic invertebrates are genuinely microscopic, well under one millimetre long. The largest is one of the two insect species, the wingless midge *Belgica antarctica*, which sometimes exceeds 10 millimetres in length. An additional hazard to life, and particularly to invertebrates which are generally drought-sensitive, is that Antarctica is the driest of the world's continents, with much of the ice-free land on the Antarctic mainland itself receiving the equivalent of around 100 millimetres or less each year in precipitation.

The short summer season is one of hectic growth, partly in the size of the individual but more evidently in numbers. Most microscopic animals reproduce rapidly anyway, and in the Antarctic (as often in other stressful environments some will reproduce by parthenogenesis, a process in which the egg does not require fertilization by a sperm to develop. Sexual reproduction is normally a slower process, but does offer the advantages of a mixing of genetic resources. The exchange of genetic material that takes place in the act of fertilization produces the variability which is the substance of adaptation and evolution in changing or challenging environments. Consequently it is rarely abandoned entirely by invertebrates (though several Nematodes fall into this category).

As in the Arctic, winter survival and the avoidance of structural damage caused by ice crystals forming within the cell are of paramount importance to invertebrates. Some, like the Tardigrades and Nematodes, seem able to lose much of their cell water and avoid disruption as they deep-freeze in this way. Others – the midges and the mites – increase the concentration of 'antifreeze' constituents in their blood, sometimes to the extent that glycerol levels may reach one per cent. The Rotifers lay thick-shelled, very tough eggs which remain dormant – often for years in succession – until suitable weather conditions provoke a hatch and rapid development to the completion of the life cycle with yet more egg laying.

The strange so-called 'freshwater' lakes and pools in the dry valleys of that part of Antarctica are normally very saline – hence they do not freeze except in the most extreme circumstances. In these pools various Copepods (rather akin to freshwater shrimps) survive and often flourish, as do Rotifers, to the extent that frequently (like some algae) their very numbers stain the water red.

The sub-Antarctic islands, cold, wet and windswept as they are, hold little more in the way of insect life. On both South Georgia and the South Shetlands, the same invertebrate groups predominate, with the insects very much in the minority. On the South Shetlands, the same two midges occur, with small dancing columns of the flying species evident, especially near the shore on comparatively warm, calm summer days. South Georgia was claimed by the ornithologist Niall Rankin to have the richest invertebrate fauna of the islands in the Scotia Arc. Rotifers, Nematodes, Collembola and so on are present in much the same orders of numbers of species, but the insects show a striking increase to five species of beetle plus four of Diptera, or flies! As with the flowering plants, by the time the latitude of the Falkland Islands has been reached, the invertebrate fauna is both far richer and more diverse. Again it shows clearly the influence of the human colonists in the large number of species that have been inadvertently introduced in one way or another – often on plants or foodstuffs. This should not be allowed to influence the general picture that the land ringing the Arctic Ocean, with the tremendous continental landmasses lying to the south, is far richer in its invertebrate fauna than the icy Antarctic Continent, ringed by stormy seas inset with only a few small windswept and extremely isolated island groups, with little lying to the north except more ocean.

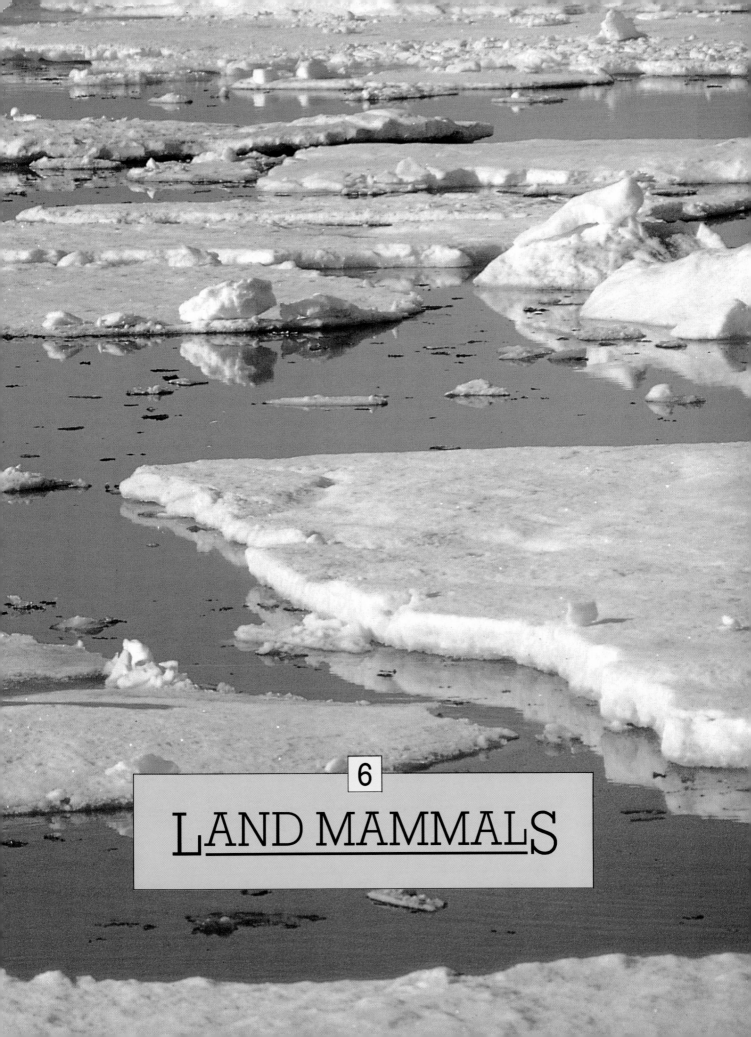

6

LAND MAMMALS

It is in the realms of the land mammals that the contrast between the north and the south polar regions is at its greatest. Indeed it could hardly be greater, as naturally-occurring terrestrial mammals are completely absent from Antartica. Even on the low-latitude sub-Antarctic archipelagos, it is feral mammal populations, originating from escapes or deliberate introductions, that dominate the scene. In contrast, in the Arctic terrestrial mammals range in size from the Lemming to the Musk Ox, and one of the Arctic predators, the Polar Bear, may even on occasion reach the North Pole itself, although most of the herbivores are naturally found at rather lower latitudes, even in summer.

The reasons for such a striking contrast are likely to be complex. Certainly the isolation of both the Antarctic Continent itself and the sub-Antarctic Islands surrounding it, which has so evidently influenced their plant life, must play a major part. But surely this cannot be the sole reason. The reasons for the comparative richness of the Arctic mammals are similarly complex, but the extensive hinterland stretching south from the circumpolar belt of tundra into temperate climates must play a large part. This creates a problem in determining which of these terrestrial mammals are essentially Arctic, and which are simply northern forms of temperate mammal, exploiting an opportunist chance to expand into the habitat. Some, too, like many of the Arctic birds, are migrants, moving north from boreal forest wintering grounds to exploit the summer richness of the tundra; the Caribou is an excellent example of this. The aim of producing a representative, rather than totally comprehensive account of terrestrial mammal life in the Arctic has guided the selection that follows.

There is a certain logic in starting with the plant-eaters, the herbivores. They are the first consumers of the plant material which forms the basis of all life, and on them the carnivores, the flesh-eating predators, ultimately depend. There is a certain logic, too, in beginning at the lower end of the size scale, particularly as the Lemming, one of the smallest terrestrial mammals, is often by far the most numerous, and in terms of the Arctic 'ecological economy' certainly a candidate for the title of 'most important' Arctic mammal.

Lemmings are best-known, perhaps notorious, for their numbers and strange behaviour in 'plague' years. Population fluctuations, with peaks in numbers roughly every four years, are marked in many small rodents, but none more so than the Lemming. If conditions are favourable, the weather mild and food abundant, their population density may reach 250 per hectare, at which times they show several behavioural anomalies. They may cease feeding, become restless, noisy and inquisitive, maybe even aggressive, and often show a strong but pointless migratory urge. Gathering hordes will press onwards blindly, non-stop, even passing through areas where food is abundant, and into the sea, marching suicidally on to almost certain death. Though this phenomenon – 'lemming-like behaviour' – has been known for centuries, it is still hardly understood.

These population peaks (and indeed their subsequent crashes) have a profound impact on Lemming predators. Towards the end of a good peak season large numbers of these will have gathered, ranging from Snowy Owls, through Pomarine and Long-tailed Skuas and Glaucous Gulls to Rough-legged Buzzards, plus Arctic Foxes. Even Polar Bears have been seen overturning boulders to get at the Lemming nests beneath. The breeding of Snowy Owls is clearly governed by Lemming numbers, the clutch size being smaller in years when numbers are low. Pomarine Skuas, too, are heavily influenced, and in years when Lemmings are most scarce they may be absent as breeding birds from large expanses of otherwise suitable tundra. By their noisy and conspicuous behaviour in peak years, Lemmings might appear to be their own worst enemies, attracting the attention of potential predators, but there is some debate as to whether their brightly-patterned fur acts as a warning colouration, alerting predators to possible unpleasant taste or aggressive behaviour. Certainly a cornered Lemming will put up a hostile and nimble defence, and there are many records of part-consumed Lemmings being regurgitated and left uneaten by predators, perhaps supporting the view that they are in some way distasteful. At lower latitudes where there is a choice between various voles and Lemmings, predators seem to select voles.

Lemmings live among the plants or just below the soil surface, making ball-shaped nests out of nearby vegetation. Often they will tunnel beneath rocks, and in winter are

PAGES 84–85: Loneliest animal on earth – a hunting Polar Bear lopes across the ice.

Lemming.

snugly insulated by the snow cover – their own igloo. Beneath the snow they may be safe from some of their predators, but Arctic Foxes seem able to locate them with little difficulty, and the Ermine (or white winter Stoat) is supple, slim and short-legged enough to be able to live in and pursue them through their own tunnel networks. On the snow surface, their high-speed waddling gait leaves a broad continuous track, quite unlike the series of paired footprints left by other small rodents which tend to hop across the snow. For food, almost all of the Arctic plants will be eaten, with mosses and lichens, and perhaps protein-rich buds, predominating in winter, while grasses, sedges and flowering plants are most important in summer.

In a good year, with favourable conditions, the first litters will be born well before the snow has thawed to any degree. Born beneath the snow, they are well insulated even in March, and it is these early litters that may suffer heavily as they are very important as a food resource to Arctic predators anxiously awaiting the return of the vast numbers of summer-visitor birds. The Lemming gestation period is around twenty days, and in good times one litter per month is achievable, with perhaps a total of six or seven litters in the year. Additionally, females can become sexually mature as early as twenty days old, and as litters can contain a dozen young, the potential for speedy multiplication is enormous! In lean years, the number of litters and the number of young each litter contains are dramatically reduced, almost to the level that the population barely ticks over, with breeding restricted to the high summer months of June and July.

Appreciably larger in size, and much more stable in population dynamics, are the northern hares. Two are of particular interest, the so-called Arctic Hare (*Lepus timidus*) which is actually far more widespread in northern Europe and North America than its name implies; in those regions it is also known as the Mountain Hare or Blue Hare, and the Snowshoe Hare of North America, *Lepus americanus*. Both species have a predominantly white winter fur, which has a double purpose. The obvious benefit of white fur as a camouflage against white snow is well understood, but the other benefit, though less well-known may actually be the greater. The white

Blue Hare in its summer coat.

'colour' of the fur is produced by the optical effect of light reflecting off a colourless, but hollow hair. Were the hair to be colourless and solid, it would be barely visible, but the inclusion of a cavity produces a reflective surface and the white appearance. More important, the cavity (as in cavity walls and double glazing) has great insulation value, and white winter fur confers appreciable benefits in heat retention. In May, or thereabouts the dense white pelage is shed, to be replaced by a thinner brown fur which also offers better summer camouflage.

Despite their size, hares in the Arctic will often live in burrows beneath the soil, seizing when available the opportunity to graze exposed vegetation on areas where the wind has drifted the snow clear. June, July and August provide comparatively easy feeding, with a wide choice of food plants, but at other times twigs of willow and birch and the various relatives of Bilberry and heather, eaten before they are much more than 5 millimetres in diameter, form the bulk of the diet. It seems that birch leaders are comparatively very rich in protein, and these are of the greatest importance in midwinter.

Certainly these foods are adequate to ensure that the females are in good enough condition to produce their litter (just one each year) in May and June, having mated in late April or early May. Each litter contains between two and five leverets (generally nearer two) and the implication of this single,

small litter compared with the huge productivity of the Lemmings is that survival rates are astonishingly high. The hares of the Arctic must be extremely well suited to their harsh environment, and perhaps fleet enough of foot to suffer only minimal predation.

In terms of adaptation to their environment, the two hares show some interesting features. Their fur has already been discussed, and it should come as no surprise to discover that the soles of their feet are densely clad in short fur as protection against the cold snow. In keeping with what is known as Bergmann's Rule (which states that the colder its surroundings, the larger and more nearly spherical an animal becomes) the more northerly Arctic Hares have a skull length of about 9 centimetres when mature, contrasting with the average of about 7 centimetres in northern Scotland for the same species. Much the same features are shown by Lemmings: in Siberia their length is on average 10 · or 11 centimetres, against a low-Arctic average of about 8 centimetres.

An associated rule – Allen's Rule – states that the further north an organism is found, the shorter will be its appendages (because it is from these limbs that heat is most easily lost). This is why the Arctic Tern has much shorter legs than its very similar temperate counterpart, the Common Tern: though in behaviour, plumage and voice the two are strikingly similar, the longer legs of the Common Tern are a valuable field identification character-

istic. So far as their ears are concerned, both Snowshoe and Arctic Hares conform to this rule by having much shorter, more rabbit-like ears than hares of temperate climates, and in the Arctic Hare, the limbs too are reduced comparatively in size. In the Snowshoe Hare, however, other evolutionary factors have intervened, and the hind feet are comparatively speaking much enlarged to give extra support on soft snow – hence the name Snowshoe.

As the snow begins to melt in May so, on the southerly fringes of the Arctic, the Caribou (or in Europe the Reindeer, in the few places where these are still wild) leave the boreal forest fringes where they have wintered and begin their long northerly migratory trek, often 500 kilometres or more, to their summer grazing grounds. They will use well-marked trails, often centuries old, and hence the concern surrounding oil pipeline laying across these ancestral routes and the provision of underpasses or bridges where necessary to avoid disruption. They feed, rest and move on relentlessly, day and night, at a steady pace unless alarmed into a panicky, rocking-horse gallop by prowling Wolves or a Wolverine. The females or cows are in the vanguard, with the bulls and yearlings following two or three weeks later. As they travel they moult from their heavy winter coat into a lighter summer one, marking their trail with tufts of stiff bristly hairs.

Through swamp and snowdrift, broadly splayed, fur-fringed hooves stop the Caribou sinking deeply, acting almost like snowshoes. These broad feet also help the Caribou to swim strongly, and they need to, as they must cross numerous fast-flowing rivers swollen with snow melt-water. Hollow hairs in their fur help here with buoyancy, as well as with warmth. The hooves themselves are sharp-edged, sharp enough to give a good grip on wet rock or on ice patches, and also sharp enough to function as powerful and effective digging tools to reach vital food plants buried beneath sudden snow or ice.

Caribou calves are normally born along the way on migration, the cow taking little more than two or three days off from her march: a longer delay would render them vulnerable to predators. The birth is rapid, and in minutes the calf is up on its feet and able to suckle. Next day, often enough, it will be able to walk on at heel, keeping up the relentless pace until the snow clears in June and the herd reaches the summer pastures in the High Arctic.

Summer brings with it relative warmth, and a plentiful and varied food supply of leaves and shoots rich in nutrients, and even fungi: all in marked contrast to the lichens, especially 'reindeer moss' that have sustained the herd through the long months of winter. It also brings with it the problems of mosquitoes and midges that seem readily able to penetrate the fur or find exposed soft parts, and the dreaded Warble Fly. So much terror does this unpleasant pest induce that often panic-stricken groups of Caribou rush into rivers or lakes to escape the scourge. Some groups of Caribou will seek escape out on windswept hilltops where the insects find life more difficult.

Both sexes in the Caribou have handsome antlers, which is unusual in the deer family. These are smaller and slimmer in the female than the male; they are shed once each year and regrown, which process separates the deer from the antelopes that retain their horns for life.

The bulls shed their antlers at the turn of the year, after the rutting season, the cows not until spring. By July, prominent buds on the forehead show the start of the next growth, which is phenomenally rapid. Soon spectacular antlers are in place, clad in 'velvet', a thick, soft skin. This velvet begins to strip off late in summer, helped by much rubbing of antlers on nearby tough vegetation. The bulls use their antlers in earnest in the autumn during the rut, when battles (a mixture of head-on collisions and rather more 'neck wrestling' with antlers interlocked) decide which of the bulls are strongest and best able to gather, and keep, a small harem of cows safe from challengers.

Autumn, too, is the time of the return migration for the Caribou. During the summer, they will have filled a vital role in the survival strategies of various Inuit tribes, which may be heavily dependent on Caribou for flesh and skins, especially useful for tent-making, as well as for clothes and kayaks. Bones and antlers make many valuable implements, ranging from knives and scrapers to fishhooks, harpoon tips, and sledge equipment.

Though the Caribou may be much the same length, the Musk Ox is by far the bulkiest of

LEFT: **Caribou show a wide range of adaptations to Arctic life** (H. Rhode).

PAGES 92–93: **Caribou on the trek.**

the Arctic herbivores. At a distance, they look like huge, slow moving, grey boulders, well camouflaged against a very rocky landscape. The Musk Ox fits well with Bergmann's and Allen's Rules, being massive with short, very stout limbs, and almost without a tail. It stands around 150 centimetres at the shoulder, with a length of 200–250 centimetres, but weighs up to 400 kilogrammes, the males being larger and heavier than the females.

Musk Oxen are tough, capable of digging down through hard-packed snow or even ice to reach the vegetation beneath, and they are extremely hardy, protected by a dense undercoat of woolly fur, covered by the fleece proper, with 50–70 centimetre long hairs giving an almost airtight outer cover and providing, altogether, excellent insulation. The long hair can on occasion constitute a major hazard: if a mid-winter warm spell produces some rainfall, this rain can freeze into an impenetrable sheet on the fur and completely immobilize the Musk Ox.

The dense winter coat must be shed early in the summer – usually in May – or the risks of overheating would be considerable. The underfur is lost first, and for much of the early summer Musk Oxen can only be described as bedraggled. They cannot sweat (in common with most hairy creatures) so they reduce their body heat by panting, or if the temperature is too high, standing deep in patches of soft snow, occasionally eating mouthfulls.

The insulation provided by the fur is augmented by a thick layer of fat laid down during the months of rich summer feeding (rather like whale blubber) which also serves as an important food reserve. In harsh winters this fatty layer may be almost used up by February, except in pregnant females. As early as July, feeding to augment the fat layer for winter will begin, concentrating heavily not just on the mixed flora of the Arctic pasture, but particularly on the very nutritious dwarf willow twigs that will also sustain the Musk Ox herd well into the winter.

The Musk Ox gets its name from the powerful smell of musk produced by a gland on the face of the bull and rubbed on to his hind legs and on to nearby vegetation, particularly during the rutting season, to mark out his territory. The scientific name, *Ovibos*,

Musk Oxen in a defensive circle *(Steve McCutcheon).*

shows the dilemma in which zoologists found themselves when trying to classify the Musk Ox, as *Ovis* is the generic name for sheep, *Bos* the generic name for cattle! Actually, the Musk Ox is related to the sheep and antelopes, and does not shed its horns each year. The males fight with these horns, which are long, curved and sharply pointed, but very massive and broad at the base, the two horn bosses meeting to give a solid horny band across the forehead. Their skulls are also unusually thick, and this and the horn bosses protect the brain from damage during rutting season challenges between bulls. These fights are spectacular in the extreme: rival bulls will face up to each other, often just a few paces apart, heads lowered before leaping forward to meet, head on, in a crash that echoes off the nearby rock faces and quite literally shakes the ground for some distance around. This may be repeated, with the length of charge increasing, ten or a dozen times before one bull backs down and trots away, often pursued by the victor.

Musk Oxen are herd animals under the control of a dominant bull – the strongest. He has in his care a number of cows and yearlings, the number effectively controlled by his ability to watch over them and look out for intruders, which may also be governed by the nature of the terrain. Up-and-coming males will be attempting to poach wayward females from the harem without necessarily fighting the dominant bull for control. If they can 'elope' to a reasonable distance without being noticed, the dominant bull is faced with a dilemma, for to pursue the escapees, he must leave the bulk of the females unguarded, and this he is normally loathe to do.

The herd has a well-developed defensive strategy, that clearly has proved effective against most predators except man. In the open they gather in a tight circle, rumps together and with an impressive array of horns pointing outwards, the calves and heifers sheltering in the centre. Summer herds may only be ten or-so animals strong, but in winter herds amalgamate to groups of fifty or more. Even in summer, this defensive circle is effective against Wolves, and it would be a desperately hungry Wolf pack indeed that tackled a large winter herd. Even a lone bull, perhaps an ageing and recently defeated elder, or a younger male who has just failed to acquire the beginnings of a harem, will use

Stoat in summer in the boreal forest fringe.

the same ploy, backing up to a cliff or even a solitary boulder to protect his flanks, and relying on that massive head and formidable pair of horns to deter attackers, usually successfully.

In the Arctic the predators range in size from the Least Weasel (little bigger than the Lemmings it hunts, but only penetrating the fringes of the Low Arctic) to the Polar Bear, largest of the Arctic land mammals and formidable indeed. Commoner than the Least Weasel, and more properly described as an Arctic predator is the Stoat. For an appreciable part of the year the Stoat is clad in its white winter coat (relieved only by the black tail tip that shows as effectively as the black spots in the white fur borders of the robes of British Peers of the Realm) and its alternative name Ermine seems almost more appropriate.

Although to human observers the Ermine's inquisitive nature and habit of raising itself up on its hind legs may be endearing, this animal is a ruthless and effective predator. For much of the year, the Ermine's main prey are the Lemmings: like the Lemmings, they can live a perfectly effective life beneath the winter snows, even protected from extremes of temperature by the insulating properties of the snow. Though they have a body length (tail included) of 30–40 centimetres and a large male may weigh up to 400 grammes or even more, the Ermine are well-adapted to the pursuit of their prey. Short legs and an extremely flexible, sinuous body reduce the

Ermine's 'head-on' size to much the same as that of a Lemming: in consequence it can hunt the Lemmings at speed through their tunnels in the vegetation or below the snow. On the snow surface Ermine leave characteristic tracks. Short legs and a comparatively long body do not make for easy progress on soft snow, so the Ermine progress by 'leaps-and-bounds' (an irregular pattern of longer or shorter hops) which gives an unevenly spaced pattern of paired footprints in the snow.

Before the tundra breeding birds of summer return, the early litters of Lemmings are most important, particularly in getting the Ermine female into good condition for the completion of her own pregnancy. Litters are born in April and May (later in the extreme north of their range) and vary from four or five to even a dozen young. This variability is closely associated with Lemming population levels – the more Lemmings, the larger the Ermine family – to the extent that in Lemming 'crash' years, with prey extremely scarce (despite the imminent arrival of the summer migrant birds) some Ermine may not breed at all.

At about the same time roaming males seek out the females and mating takes place. After the young are born, the female must be at pains to conceal her litter from the male, particularly if food is in short supply, for he would have little compunction in eating them. At this time (and partly at least for this reason) the female will move her den often, carrying her youngsters like kittens one by one by the scruff of the neck to a fresh hole beneath a convenient rock. The female and youngsters stay together throughout the Arctic summer, the youngsters learning the skills of hunting first by observation and then by practical experience. Studies in Low Arctic habitats have indicated that female territories range from 5–10 hectares, while the male may roam over four times this area, but this home range is also very heavily dependent on Lemming numbers.

The Ermine, *Mustela erminea*, is the same species as that occurring over much of the temperate zone of the Northern Hemisphere, but more special to the Low Arctic, particularly the boreal forest fringes, is its larger relative in the Mustelid family, the Wolverine, which at a length of about one metre and a weight of up to 25 kilogrammes, is one of the largest Mustelids. The Wolverine looks like a small bear, with legs of much more normal proportion than the Ermine. Its build is strong, even powerful, and its feet are relatively large, useful to prevent the Wolverine sinking in soft snow as it moves, almost always at a loping gallop. Most are dark brown or blackish, with a paler yellowish band round the buttocks and with indistinct, almost Badger-like pale markings on the head. Unlike the Ermine, this brownish fur is maintained year round, save for bleaching slightly during the summer. The coat is of high quality in furrier's terms, but more practically, seems not to collect the ice crystals inevitably formed as warm breath meets the cold Arctic winter air. These ice crystals are a painful and often dangerous problem to the Eskimo people (who are beardless) and to Arctic trappers and explorers, whose beards quickly become encrusted. With clothing, on entering a warm tent or igloo, the ice crystals melt, making fur hoods soggy, only to freeze rigidly when next exposed to the open air. Consequently, Wolverine skins are much in demand among the Eskimo peoples, particularly for the pragmatic purpose of lining the hoods of their parkas.

Wolverines are solitary animals, and usually meet others only to mate during the summer. As in the case of the Ermine, implantation of the embryo is often delayed until late autumn, and the young (usually two or three of them) are born in mid-winter – usually February or March. The female digs a den deep in a large snowdrift, and in the warmth and protection this offers the young pass their early weeks. As the weather improves in spring, they will begin to join the female on training hunting forays. This will last until autumn, when male cubs will wander off to begin their solitary existence, though female cubs may remain some months longer with their mother. Females are thought to mature in their second year, males probably later in life. Breeding is normally an annual event, but both litter size, and whether they breed at all, can be influenced by extreme food scarcity.

Though they are extremely catholic in their diet, Wolverines have enormous home ranges. Some studies have indicated that females may routinely cover a territory of between 50 and 300 square kilometres, while males may range over 1,000 square kilometres, overlapping the territories of several

females. It is the female who most closely defends a territory, particularly in spring when she has the young to feed, scent-marking copiously around its boundaries to warn off other females in particular, while of course attracting and identifying herself to any wandering potential male suitor.

Despite the variety of their diet, which takes prey of all sizes from birds' eggs and young, and Lemmings upwards, as well as berries in autumn, the Wolverines major prey is the Caribou or Reindeer. This is especially the case in winter, when the Caribou herds have retreated from the tundra to the forest margins. Caribou prey may be as carrion –the result of an accident, or starvation, or indeed the 'left-overs' of a kill made by Wolves or a Brown Bear. But Wolverines are relentless hunters in their own right, able to pursue their selected victim for many kilometres without tiring. They are particularly successful when the snow conditions are in their favour: in soft, powdery snow their gait, shortish leg-length and large feet serve them better than the

long-legged Caribou, whose broad feet seem to impede it even further as it flounders through deep snow. Calculations show that in these circumstances, the Caribou exerts something like ten times as much pressure per square centimetre on the snow as does the Wolverine.

Once a kill has been made, the Wolverine speedily dismembers its victim. Some of the flesh is eaten on the spot, resulting in a great deal of blood on the snow, but most is taken off and hidden, cached (as a squirrel conceals nuts) to be relocated later in the winter when times are hard. The size of its kills, the apparently bloodthirsty manner in which the victim is subsequently butchered, and the habit of hiding away what cannot be eaten on the spot (a very sensible adaptation for survival in the harsh Arctic-fringe winter) have given the Wolverine an evidently undeserved reputation for greediness, and the alternative name 'Glutton'.

If the Ermine and the Wolverine are not Arctic 'specialities', the one because of its

Greediest of the Arctic animals by reputation, the Wolverine.

widespread temperate distribution, the other because it penetrates only the forested fringes of the Low Arctic, then the Arctic Fox certainly is. Amongst other things, its winter coat is of such length, thickness and structure that it has been measured as offering better insulation against the bitter cold of the Arctic winter than the fur of any other mammal. Particularly for the white form, hollow hairs confer the 'whiteness' that provides such effective camouflage against sparklingly clear winter snowscapes, as well as additional insulation properties. This has obviously led to the popularity of the Arctic Fox for the manufacture of furs for human adornment. As the winter fur is appreciably denser than the summer, trapping is a winter activity, but the cruelty involved is impossible to support. Not only is the trapping of an animal by the leg in toothed, heavily sprung, steel jaws barbaric, but equally horrific is leaving it to die slowly when bad weather prevents the trapper regularly visiting his trap lines. The alternative route of fox farming – raising Arctic Foxes in captivity purely for their skins – finds some supporters, but the weight of public opinion is now firmly behind the cessation of the use of animal furs for human clothing, with the exception perhaps of clothing for Eskimo tribespeople, where natural furs excel in several qualities over any man-made alternative.

Other adaptations of the Arctic Fox to its climate, minimizing heat loss, include (compared with the temperate foxes) relatively rotund, plump bodies, with short legs, a short tail, and a very round face, with ears and muzzle much shorter and therefore appreciably less 'foxy' and more appealing to the human eye. The feet are well adapted too, with hairy undersides to relatively large paws which are referred to in the specific name *Alopex lagopus. Lagopus* is a compound of two Greek words: 'lagos' meaning hair and 'pous' meaning foot. Interestingly, the Ptarmigan, one of the best Arctic-snow-adapted birds, has feathering on the undersides of its feet as well as on its legs and has the generic name *Lagopus*.

Arctic Foxes are unusual – possibly unique – amongst mammals of the Northern Hemisphere in occurring in two different colour varieties or morphs. Commoner and more widespread is the morph which is brownish grey over most of its body, save for a pale greyish-white chest and belly, during the summer, and totally white during the winter months. The other morph, the 'Blue Fox' of the fur trade, is much darker, and as its name implies, blue-grey: a colour that persists right through the year. The benefits – or indeed the disadvantages – of these two morphs are imperfectly understood, but clearly the white winter morph benefits against the snowy background of winter. In these conditions the blue morph would be at a disadvantage, but it seems that most blue foxes occur in coastal areas, feeding a lot on the shore, where their dull fur confers better camouflage and where the marginally milder climate may put them at less of a disadvantage. The two forms overlap in occurrence in many areas, and there seems to be no colour selection by the female in the choice of her mate.

Arctic Fox dens are features of the landscape: many have been in existence for decades, perhaps centuries, and the visiting eye is compulsively drawn to them because the surrounding vegetation is so strange. Years of the depositing of droppings and food remains around the many tunnel entrances to the dens have enriched the soil not only in nitrates but also in phosphates, so a comparatively luxuriant range of plants flourishes, with dark green foliage the most striking feature. During the early spring, the vixen will be visited in her den by a number of roving dog foxes, and by May or June, a litter of cubs will be born, but only in years when sufficient Lemmings are available. In 'crash' years, and perhaps for a year or two after, many Arctic Foxes will not breed at all, while in 'plague' years litters of a dozen or more cubs can be raised in a healthy state.

Abstinence – from breeding in low-Lemming years and from feeding in times of hardship – must be a paramount feature of Arctic Fox life. Though they are extremely unselective in their diet, relishing everything from the most aged and unappetizing carrion, including leathery fragments of skin, through berries in autumn and seashore molluscs (which they quickly learn to hunt at low tide), to the plentiful supplies of summer breeding birds, their eggs and their nestlings, they depend very heavily on supplies of Lemmings. These they catch with a nimble, cat-like, leaping pounce, pinning the Lemming down beneath the front paws before snapping it into the jaws. When Lemming numbers

LEFT: **Arctic Fox.**

are low, winter for Arctic Foxes must be a period of extreme hardship, and they seem able to endure many days, even weeks of starvation.

Perhaps most familiar to us in the guise of its domestic descendant – the Alsatian or German Shepherd dog – the Wolf, an appreciably larger relative of the Arctic Fox, is one of nature's most adaptable animals. It has occurred in every habitat in the Northern Hemisphere, including the desert fringes, and including the Arctic, though in the last three or four centuries its distribution has been much reduced under the influence of persecution by mankind. The Wolf is essentially a pack animal, socially very well organized, and perhaps because of this its choice of prey centres heavily on larger animals, though carrion and the occasional Lemming or vole are rarely ignored.

In the Low Arctic it is the Caribou (or Reindeer) that is the staple item in the diet of polar Wolf packs. Usually it seems that an individual member of the Caribou herd is selected as a target, and several researches have shown this individual almost always to be either unusually young, or aged, or infirm. Once selected, the victim will be relentlessly pursued, though flee it might, with various members of the Wolf pack taking turns in making the running and therefore prolonging the collective staying power of the pack as a whole. Once their quarry is cornered or brought to bay, though it will defend itself vigorously with its antlers and razor-sharp hooves, weight of numbers eventually begins to tell, first with a few disabling bites to the legs and hindquarters, then with the killing bite to the throat. Once a kill has been made, the pack eats its fill, paying due attention to the social structure which affords priority to the lead male, his senior bitches, and to any female which is feeding cubs. This well-developed social structure is in part responsible for the vocal activities of Wolf packs, as many of the howling and wailing cries are contact messages either within the pack or between packs. Though these howls are calculated to strike chill horror into the heart of humans, and indeed though Wolves are a frequent focus of horror films, actual Wolf attacks on man are an extremely rare event indeed.

Wolf society is complex: there is a hierarchy amongst the males within the pack,

determining that only the current pack leader mates with the bitches, while the others play a supportive role in hunting and in defence of the pack. Until, that is, they feel that their turn has come, and they attempt to oust the leader in a show of threat or occasionally actual force. Not only that, but amongst the bitches there is also a pecking order with the most senior receiving the extra favours. Most bitches will be mature at two years old, many will not mate for the first time until they are at least three, often four. Non-breeding bitches

A lone Wolf samples the scents of the boreal forest edge.

join non-breeding males as the work-force of the pack. Various animals within the pack will help bring food to suckling bitches when they pup in April onwards, depending on latitude and season, mating having taken place in late winter. After some sixty days gestation, the bitch will give birth to a litter of six or more cubs: the number of bitches breeding, and the size of their litters, is generally related to prey availability, but to nowhere near the striking degree shown by Ermine, Arctic Foxes, and those avian predators also heavily dependent on Lemmings and their violent fluctuation in numbers.

Nor is there any evidence to suggest that Polar Bears, the largest and most powerful of the Arctic land predators, show population fluctuations common to the smaller carnivores. More than any other bear, and no doubt due to its extreme habitat, the Polar Bear has adapted to a diet almost entirely of flesh, including occasional fish, birds and the young of any other animal it may encounter, including tiny ones like Lemmings, but primarily composed of seals. Carrion, particularly in the form of a stranded whale, is never passed by. Records suggest that gorging when food is plentiful is the Polar Bear's normal habit, with up to 40 kilogrammes of flesh being eaten at one sitting!

Polar Bears may reach almost 3 metres in length and 800 kilogrammes in weight, the males being considerably larger than the females. When hunting, very sensitive powers of scent are backed up by phenomenal persistence, patience and physical endurance – sufficient to wait long hours beside a seal's blow-hole, maintaining not just vigilance but instant reaction, for the lethal paw-strike and bite must be made in seconds of the return of the seal after a forty-minute dive. Though they swim powerfully in the ice-cold sea, they never hunt while doing so because seals in the water are in the element of which they are the masters, at their fastest and most agile, whilst on land they are slow and awkward, ready prey to the surprisingly fast, loping gallop of a hunting bear. When swimming, Polar Bears 'dog-paddle' with their broad and strong front paws, using their hind legs held together as a rudder with which to steer.

White hollow-haired fur insulates the Polar Bear in the same effective way, year-round, as it does other Arctic mammals. A dense undercoat keeps insulation properties high, protected by a longer outer coat of guard hairs which stick together when wet to form a waterproof barrier. Beneath the fur is a layer of blubber comparable in thickness to that of a seal: this fatty layer serves the double purpose of additional insulation and a reserve food store, to be drawn on and metabolized during leaner times. Polar Bears do not hibernate as do some of the northern Brown Bear species: many males will hunt without ceasing right through the long, dark Arctic winter, only sheltering during the worst of blizzards. This sheltering is easily achieved: the bear merely curls up, nose and head buried deep in the fur of its flanks, and allows an insulating snowdrift to form around it.

Females protect themselves rather more, and may spend periods of several days at a time dozing, deep in a snow cave dug in a drift. Having mated with a roaming male back in March or April, the fertilized egg is retained (without further development) in the oviduct, and its implantation in the fleshy wall of the uterus (where it will begin to develop into an embryo) is delayed until the autumn. The youngsters, often one, sometimes twins, are born at around New Year, sheltered within the snow cave. This is just as well, as at birth they are helpless and tiny, at a few hundred grams scaling perhaps only one thousandth of their mother's weight! Growth after birth is fast, as with a 30 per cent fat content Polar Bear milk is richer than that of any other land carnivore. The cubs will remain with their mother for at least a year or more of valuable schooling in the ways and means of survival in Arctic circumstances, male cubs generally setting off on an independent life before females.

Hunting has to be *the* major factor in the life of a Polar Bear. Though summer may produce riches in the way of bird life, easily caught, this can only be considered as a snack, and anyway it is only available for a brief part of each year. The mainstay of their diet is the Ringed Seal, present in the Arctic, well up towards the North Pole itself, year-round. But this is a solitary seal: why does not the Polar Bear favour the much more gregarious Harp Seal? The answer is two-fold: certainly if a Polar Bear comes across a breeding colony of Harp Seals on the moving ice fields, it will wreak havoc, slaughtering seals left, right and centre, taking only the odd bite here and there, playing with seal pups as a cat plays with a mouse. But Harp Seals shift their breeding grounds each year, and anyway are on floating, often moving ice, so it will only be by chance that a Polar Bear stumbles across one of their colonies. Rather, the Polar Bear lies (often prone), vigilant, close to a patch of open sea or a blow-hole. Should a Ringed Seal surface, it is swiftly seized, killed and dragged out before it sinks from reach. Such is the power of a Polar Bear that once grasped, a Ringed Seal can be pulled in its entirety through the breathing hole in ice perhaps some metres thick. The hole may only be the diameter of its head, so this process forcibly dislocates or breaks most of the bones in the seal's body.

Thus the Polar Bear is a purpose-built hunter of immense power. As it leads a largely solitary life in the Arctic wilderness, it must also be perhaps the loneliest animal on earth, as well as perhaps the most northerly, for tracks and droppings have been found within a few kilometres of the North Pole itself.

RIGHT: The polar bear cuts a dramatic figure on a stranded iceberg in the Arctic.

7

MARINE MAMMALS

Because of the relative uniformity of the habitat in which they live, it is amongst the marine mammals that similarities become much more evident than contrasts in comparing the two polar regions. There *are* some differences however: obvious ones (though minor) include the different species of whales and seals involved; and more subtle ones include the lack of land predators on seals in the Antarctic. But none of these serve to produce the striking contrasts that are so obvious in the plant life and in the rest of polar animal life between the two regions.

Both polar regions hold a number of seal species, and several whales, but it is only in the Arctic that the Walrus flourishes – as two species, the Northern Pacific one being slightly larger than its North Atlantic close relative. During the Arctic winter, these huge members of the seal family tend to wander, usually in small groups. Often they will come

ashore, when, though they may be gregarious, they are smelly and extremely noisy: the roars of the bulls are far-carrying, especially over ice, as they indulge in combat, both mock and real, for the favours of the females. The gestation period is roughly twelve months, so the young are born early in the summer on boulder-strewn beaches. In marked contrast to the seals, the youngsters are suckled by their cows for some two years, so the females breed every third year at best.

On rocky Low Arctic islands, their very presence is destructive to vegetation and soil; especially if the males are fighting, their great bulk humping about causes a great deal of damage. Others will spend the winter close to the edge of stable sea ice – here rough seas tend to prevent sudden extensive freezing of large sea areas, and the Walrus has enough weight and strength to break up freshly-formed ice. Often, like seals, they will float vertically, nose up, bobbing rather like mon-

PAGES 104–105: **Giants of their family, bull Southern Elephant Seals indulge in a sparring match – but fights in earnest will soon follow.**

BELOW: **Walruses.**

Smallest of Arctic animals, the zooplankton. Their diversity is far greater than that of their much larger vertebrate relatives, with the larvae of many species of sea urchins, worms, molluscs and crustaceans well represented
(D. P. Wilson).

strous bottles while they sleep. Walruses are usually cautious when it comes to going ashore, and groups will bob around for some time inspecting the coast to see that it is clear before hauling themselves out. This they accomplish on ice with more grace than might be expected in the circumstances. Rough pads on the fore-limbs, and frequent use of the tusks to gain purchase help towards this.

The prime use of the long, strong, and slightly curved, paired tusks is to plough up the muddy sea bed. Walruses feed on large, mud-dwelling shellfish, usually bivalve molluscs like clams but occasionally also large cockle species found at depths from 50 to 100 metres. Once they have dislodged these from the bottom, they float up towards the surface, crushing the shells between the rough pads on their fore-flippers as they go. As they move about, the mud and fragments of shell sink away, leaving the flesh floating free, to be swallowed by the Walrus. As a secondary use, the tusks function effectively in defence. There are many (perhaps apocryphal) Inuit stories of Polar Bears being found with stab punctures, and certainly records of Walruses being attacked by Killer Whales are surprisingly few. The Walrus's immensely thick leathery skin must also help, but both Polar Bear and Killer Whale are persistent and powerful adversaries, terrorizing predators on seals (and, in the case of the Killer Whale, on other whales), which implies that the Walrus carries a more positive and potent means of defence.

When feeding, Walrus-dives often extend beyond ten minutes - far in excess of human diving capacity. As in the whales and seals, aeons of evolution have shaped the Walrus's ability to cope. The oxygen-carrying capacity of their blood haemoglobin is roughly half as great again as that of a comparable land mammal. Once a dive is under way, the heart-beat slows from about 150 per minute to an economic 10 per minute, and the blood supply to the body in general is restricted, with flow being maintained particularly to the lungs and brain. Metabolism slows appreciably, and body temperatures may drop as low as five per cent. The major vein along the backbone is elastic, and steadily accumulâtes deoxygenated blood. This allows an 'oxygen debt' to build up in the tissues during the dive, with a rapid replenishment when the Walrus surfaces for air.

Zoologists specializing in palaeontology – the study of fossil forms of animal life dating from pre-history – are certain that the whales and seals have evolved from mammalian

A Walrus dwarfed by the scale of the ice-floes off Ellesmere Island, Canadian Arctic.

ancestors. The seals (and sea-lions and Walruses) are carnivores grouped in the order Pinnepedia: earliest fossils date from the Miocene epoch of twenty to twenty-five million years ago, but because of their extreme adaptation to a specialized environment, their relationships with other carnivores are far from clear. One line of thought sees similarities with the bears, another with otters – but this latter may be largely due to both groups of animals exploiting the same environment, an evolutionary situation called Convergence. The whales are also thought to have originated from carnivore stock, but much further

in evidence. Thus these groups of carnivores have had an appreciable time, in evolutionary terms, to come to an adaptive harmony with their environment, although the seals and Walruses are only partly aquatic – they do emerge on to land regularly, and in particular to give birth to their young. The only truly aquatic mammals are the whales and the strange sea-cows and dugongs of the order Sirenia.

Of the large marine mammals, it is clearly the whales that have evolved the most specialized adaptations to their harsh environment. Water is a denser medium in which to live than air – think of the problems in running chest-high through even a calm sea compared with an athletics track. Mammals all depend on air for vital oxygen, obtained through the process of respiration using lungs. Unlike fish, whales cannot make use of the oxygen dissolved in water: having adopted a marine existence, they must surface to breathe at regular intervals. With their ability to dive deeply, and for long periods, it is in this area that their adaptations seem most impressive when viewed by terrestrial mankind.

As an additional hostile factor, cold seas will absorb the heat from a warm-blooded swimming mammal far faster than will the air, a fact readily validated by comparing the human swimmer with the sunbather on the adjacent beach. In the extremely cold seas of the polar regions, often (because of their salinity) at temperatures below freezing point, a fisherman or whaler unfortunate enough to fall overboard – even fully clothed – would survive only a few minutes before succumbing to exposure, yet this is the all-day, every day, habitat of several species of whales and seals.

There are, though, obvious benefits to be derived from mastering the adversities of this environment. It contains much animal life, from minute zooplankton, through shrimps like krill, to a wide range of fish. All of these may be present in vast numbers, a formidable food resource with few competitors compared with terrestrial habitats. Also, the very density of the water, although in some ways impeding movement, does through its natural buoyancy offset the weight problems of a large animal. The Blue Whale – one of the baleen whales and a krill feeder – is on record at around 30 metres in length and

back in time at some fifty million years ago in the Eocene epoch. The earliest whales were slimmer and more sea-serpent like than those of today, and probably nowhere near so efficient when swimming, though already the hind limbs had disappeared and the typical huge skull, with the nostril set well back, was

The bleached skeleton of a massive, long-dead Blue Whale on King George Island in the Antarctic.

weighing upwards of 150 tonnes, which makes this species by some degree the largest animal ever to have lived on the Earth. The seals must strike a compromise on size, as part of their existence is out of the water, and thus must be much smaller than the larger whales. Many whales are able to reach a size that would be physically unsupportable, even self-destructive, were they to live on dry land.

To live in water efficiently makes demands on both shape and skeletal structure, hence the approximately torpedo-like shape shared by whales of all sizes, seals and the vast majority of fishes – and used by man for many underwater vehicles, like submarines. Such streamlining greatly reduces the 'drag' of the water, a process helped in the case of the whales by their extremely smooth skin. Interestingly, several have a bulbous nose (thought to accommodate navigational organs), and most of these, like the Pilot Whale, are fast swimmers: it may be no coincidence that modern shipping designers

have adopted the same bulbous form for the bows of ships.

In the seals and sea-lions, the limbs still have some semblance to those of other mammals, and an examination of the bone structure within shows a skeleton of the typical pentadactyl (five-fingered) pattern, familiar from mice to men, only heavily shaped (in compression and flattening) by evolution to form an equivalent to the fish's fin. In whales this process has been more extreme, but the basic pattern is still there to see. While all fish have their tail fins set in a vertical plane, and propel themselves by side-to-side waves of muscular action, the whales, dolphins and porpoises have their tail flukes in a horizontal plane. This is the instant way of identifying them from larger fish like sharks. They achieve propulsion by waves of muscular activity in a vertical plane, much like a swimmer performing the butterfly stroke.

Power for propulsion comes solely from the tail and its flukes in the whales: the fore-limbs serve to give depth and directional control. In such a cold marine environment, having appendages of minimum length serves to reduce heat loss to a minimum, much as is the case with the polar land mammals and birds. Large bulk helps to reduce heat loss too, as the bulkier the body and the nearer it resembles a sphere in shape, the less is its surface skin area (where the heat is lost) in relation to its volume.

Obviously, though, whales and seals could not exist in such an environment with an anatomy akin to ours: they are warm-blooded, and keep their body temperature close to 37°C. Heat loss is substantially reduced by a thick layer of fat in the skin – called blubber. Ironically, it is this life-preserving insulating layer that has nearly caused the extinction of several whales, for it was this blubber that the whalers were seeking to render down into oil. Depending on the size of the whale, and its species and habitat, the blubber layer ranges from a few centimetres up to half a metre in thickness. Effective as this insulating layer is at keeping *out* the cold, problems could arise – either in warmer seas or indeed in cold seas during bursts of hunting activity or prolonged swimming – when the whale could run severe risks of overheating because bodily heat was so effectively kept *in*.

To counter this risk, a substantial network of blood vessels, under nervous and muscular control, runs through the blubber just beneath the skin surface. If there is an over-heating risk, more blood is automatically exposed to the cooling sea – a process functioning in much the same way as a car radiator.

More hazardous might be the loss of heat through the fins, which lack the insulating layer of blubber. One way of coping with this problem is to reduce their size, but clearly, if they are to function effectively in swimming, this evolutionary size-reduction process can only be carried out to a degree. In the whales, a process called 'countercurrent heat exchange' has evolved, on which sophisticated commercial heat exchangers are based. Each artery to an extremity carries warm, oxygen-rich blood under high pressure, and each is surrounded by an intricate network of low-pressure veins, which collect the used, deoxygenated blood to return it to the lungs. As the arterial blood approaches the fluke muscles, so its temperature falls as it warms the chilled blood emerging in the veins from those same tissues. At the extremities of the flukes, the blood temperature may be at about 4°C compared with the 37°C in the lungs: by pre-cooling the warm arterial blood,

Pilot Whales occasionally strand themselves in the low Arctic – then the Inuit reap an easy and rich harvest of meat *(Peter Reynolds).*

heat loss when this reaches the extremities is minimized; by simultaneously pre-warming the lung-bound blood (which would have to be warmed anyway) precious energy is saved. The balance can be altered if a cooling effect is necessary to counteract bodily overheating, and this happens automatically – altogether an intriguing and extremely effective mechanism.

With the problems encountered by human divers in mind, an obvious question to ask is how do the marine mammals avoid 'the bends', which without extreme caution in the ascent from deep dives can cripple or kill a human diver. Recent work with automatic depth recorders glued to whales and seals has produced staggering information on the frequency, duration and depth of their dives. Sperm Whales may be able to remain submerged for almost two hours, in contrast to the Rorqual of the Arctic, where forty minutes seems about the limit, and to many of the smaller porpoises and dolphins, where dives may last for only a few minutes.

It is now thought, based on depth recorder readings, that Sperm Whales may dive even deeper than the 2,000 metres suspected (because of the depth distribution of the prey items – large squids in the main – in their stomachs, revealed when they were cut open on whaling ships). Today, 3,000 metres – 3 kilometres – seems likely to be achieved with regularity by Sperm Whales, and very recent evidence indicates that this phenomenal depth may also be matched by the Elephant Seal.

To achieve such deep dives, some form of buoyancy control would seem a necessity as an energy-saving strategy. In the whales, it is argued by some authorities that the sperm oil, or spermaceti, which occupies much of the monstrous bulbous head of the Sperm Whale serves this function. On cooling, this spermaceti is transformed from a light oil to solidified fat, and as it may amount to as much as ten per cent of the body weight of a Sperm Whale, it could well be that this solidification (which would occur as the whale dived into deeper, and thus colder, water) could effectively change the buoyancy of the whale.

'The bends' are thought to be induced in human divers because they breathe compressed air. With time and depth, the supposedly inert atmospheric gas nitrogen gradually dissolves in the blood. It can be released, with crippling effects, as bubbles in the blood (just as in a bottle of lemonade bubbles form as the pressure is released by the unscrewing of the cap) if the ascent from the depths is too rapid. But whales dive after holding their breath – that is, they take down with them only the air that is in their lungs at the time, with the comparatively small amount of nitrogen that it contains. This, though, is thought only to be a part of the answer, and a fascinating field of research still awaits detailed exploration before a final solution can be found.

As any swimming-pool diver knows, 'breath-hold' diving, even in shallow water, can cause other problems, notably sharp pains in the ears as the pressure on the eardrum from outside exceeds that within the middle ear. In whales, such problems are avoided by filling veins within the middle ear – elastic ones called sinuses – with blood, thus eliminating almost all the air space and replacing it with basically incompressible blood. On diving, this protective mechanism comes into operation automatically.

Considering the duration of their dives, the whales, surfacing often just for a moment to 'blow' and refill their lungs with oxygen, recharge their systems with this vital gas with astonishing efficiency. For this purpose, the blow-hole, situated on top of the head, is ideally placed. In both whales and seals, the nostrils are held *closed* by a purse-string-like sphincter muscle, to be opened only when it is necessary to breathe – a marked contrast to other mammals but an extremely practical element of their evolution.

Whales do not have extraordinarily large lungs: in fact almost the reverse, with the deepest-diving species having the smallest lungs, so it would appear that this respiratory efficiency does not depend on lung volume. However, most whales (and seals) do have (at ten to fifteen per cent of body weight) appreciably more blood than other mammals (humans have about seven per cent for example). In addition, the numbers of red blood corpuscles that transport the oxygen, and their haemoglobin (in which it is carried) content, are appreciably greater than in other mammals. An abundance also of muscular haemoglobin (called myoglobin) gives whale muscle an excellent oxygen-carrying capacity, as well as causing the characteristic very dark colour of whale meat.

Coupled with this specialized blood is a dramatic drop in heartbeat rate during dives, often only half the rate when the whale is at the surface. This helps reduce oxygen consumption, but theoretical physiological calculations of oxygen-use over a prolonged dive show that the increased oxygen-carrying capacity of the blood *and* the low heartbeat rate can in no way account for the duration of the dive. Other processes must come into play, as with the Walrus. Blood flow to brain and heart is given priority and maintained, while that to stomach, kidneys and liver is much reduced. Deoxygenated blood is stored in inflated veins or sinuses throughout the body cavity until the whale surfaces. A fascinating, and as yet not understood, feature of whale anatomy that may also be involved are large, complex networks of blood vessels close to the spine and ribs. These are called *retia mirabile* (literally 'wonderful nets') and may serve as reservoirs of oxygenated blood for the brain, or as a pressure-equalizing 'shock-absorber' to prevent damage to the blood system during dives, or indeed poss-

ibly as a component of the 'bends' avoidance mechanism.

These adaptations in physique and in physiology must be accompanied by some extraordinary developments in sensory processes if the marine mammals are to exploit their environment to the full. In the semi-terrestrial seals these are not developed to any particularly unusual degree on superficial examination, but the navigational and hunting abilities of some Arctic seals able to flourish beneath the ice-cap, with blow-holes few and far between during the almost total darkness of the winter, must indicate some special sensory perception.

Seals, and to a lesser extent, whales, need to be able to see well out of the water. In the case of the seals, this determines the design of the eye, which is basically to the roughly spherical pattern shared by man, dog or bear. Beneath the water surface things are different and the terrestrial eye finds difficulty in focusing. The eye of a whale is a very different shape, elliptical rather than spherical, with the shortest axis fore-and-aft, from pupil through the lens to the retina. The lens of a whale eye, too, has exceptional flexibility: strong muscles take advantage of this and change the shape of the lens drastically from vision in air to vision under the sea. Whales must be able to see in bright sunshine, but also in the extreme gloom of the depths, though below 200 metres little light remains, and it is uncertain just how useful its eyes are. To restrict the bright light on the surface, the whale eye pupil is reduced to a tiny slit.

Of the other senses, the whale seems to have little sense of smell, but as might be expected because of the aquatic medium in which it lives, a very well-developed sense of taste – though this is nowhere near so acute as that of many fishes: the notorious shark family, for example.

Touch, too, is well developed – but not in the fingertip sense, as much of the sensory function of the limbs, so familiar to us, has been lost as these have developed into such specialized organs of locomotion. The entire skin is very sensitive, not just to touch but possibly more to the subtleties of the passage of water over it. In this way, the whale can adjust its speed and 'trim' to maximize its underwater efficiency. So too, can sensitive skin areas around the blow-hole be used to tell the whale when it is safe to open the 'nostril' and breathe – not an easy matter to judge by eye when the nostril is on top of the head and distant from the eye level. As in the seals, the nostril is held tightly closed, the purse-string-like muscles surrounding it opening on positive nervous command.

Sound travels slowly in water, and in the interests of streamlining, the external ear of the whale has vanished. The ear hole is often tiny, sometimes closed by a waxy plug, and much argument surrounds how much, or how little, whales use this genuine organ of hearing.

Echolocation is an altogether different matter, particularly in the toothed whales. Some experts would suggest that the use of sound communication in echolocation is one of the most sensitive and sophisticated of any sensory faculty in the animal kingdom. Mankind's recently developed sonic scanners produce images that are thought to be extremely coarse and crude compared with the 'sound picture' that a toothed whale receives of its environment.

Echolocation depends on the emission of sounds, basically as bursts of clicking noises, and on the collection and analysis of these sounds as reflected – in varying degrees – by objects in the whale's path. The sounds used may be both high and low frequency, and convey back a picture in three dimensions, with clear indications of variations in the nature and substance of the object under scrutiny.

Some scientists consider that the huge fat deposits in the heads of the toothed whales, not used, so far as is known, in metabolism (but perhaps of use in controlling buoyancy) are of such unusual chemical composition, and are positioned so strangely in front of the brain, that they may form an important part of the echolocating system. Many of the toothed whales have a markedly bulbous forehead, wherein lies the fatty deposit (called the 'melon') and it is thought that this functions almost as a lens, focusing the sound into a directional beam. In the lower jaw, another fatty deposit is thought to receive reflected sound pulses and to transmit these, via the internal ear structure, to the brain for interpretation. The brain is comparatively large, perhaps to allow for this. Certainly all the evidence points to toothed whales receiving such an accurate picture that deep-sea hunting becomes relatively easy. This would answer the old whalers' questions as to just how, with often relatively few teeth, these hunting whales located and caught their squid prey in darkness – without resorting to magic.

Much debate surrounds the question of whether or not the whalebone or baleen whales are similarly endowed with an echolocating sense. If they do have one, it seems most likely that it is much more primitive, but even so it may well be of some use in detecting major changes in the configuration of the sea floor, or indeed perhaps accumulations of prey, like krill. Most of the baleen whales use comparatively low frequency sounds to produce complex 'songs', strangely beautiful to the human ear. In the sea, these can be transmitted enormous distances, perhaps even hundreds of kilometres, but their purpose is thought to be communication, rather than navigation. Even so, none has evolved the sound range of the Beluga or White Whale, known to the whalers as the 'sea canary'.

Our knowledge, both as to the mechanism and the accuracy of echolocation as a navigational, hunting and general environmental sensor system, is obviously fragmentary, but our marvelling should not stop short at echolocation. It seems, from accumulating evidence, that whales – and possibly other animals – may well be able to perceive changes in the earth's magnetic field and use this knowledge as a sophisticated navigational aid. Some of the toothed whales have been found to have magnetic crystals in their brain tissue, and these will align themselves like magnets to the lines of magnetic force round the globe. Such a system would be largely independent of the weather and of such contrasts as night and day, sunshine or cloud, that could influence other theories on navigation. It would, though, be vulnerable to occasional geomagnetic anomalies, areas where the natural shape of the earth's magnetic field is severely distorted, perhaps by some local geological formation. It is now thought that such anomalies may contribute to the occasional live strandings of whales, and their seemingly suicidal persistence in obeying their senses and returning again and again to the same beach, despite extensive rescue operations.

Whales, called the Cetacea, as a group embrace about seventy-five species, including those normally called porpoises and dolphins. They are divided into two major and strikingly different groups. Smaller in number, but normally greater in physical size, are the Mysticeti, the baleen or whalebone whales, named after the huge brush-like baleen or whalebone sheets that fringe the edges of their cavernous mouths in place of teeth. These whalebone plates serve to filter small planktonic animals like krill from enormous gulps of sea, in sufficient quantity to keep these gigantic creatures well fed. The Mysticeti include the Grey Whales (*Eschrichtidae*), the Blue and Rorqual Whales (*Balaenopteridae*) and the Right and Bowhead Whales (*Balaenidae*). All have disproportionately monstrous heads and mouths, associated with their feeding techniques.

Of the other group, the toothed whales or Odontoceti, only the Sperm Whale has this comparatively large head, associated with its deposits of spermaceti oil. The Odontoceti include the porpoises (*Phocoenidae*), the dolphins (*Delphinidae*), and various small related groups, with the Monodontidae (the Beluga or White Whale and the Narwhal from

the Arctic), the Pilot and Killer Whales (*Globicephalidae* – named after the bulbous appearance of their heads caused by the echolocating 'melon') and the Sperm Whales (*Physeteridae*). All have peg-like teeth, sometimes in both jaws, sometimes only in one; sometimes numerous, as in the porpoises, sometimes extraordinarily developed, as in the Narwhal's single tusk. It was these teeth, especially from the Sperm Whale, that early whalers used to engrave with pictures, particularly of polar scenery, whale hunts and sailing ships, to while away long hours of waiting – a hobby called scrimshaw.

In the Arctic quite obviously the numbers of marine mammals are far less today than they were only a few centuries ago. This diminution in numbers is largely the result of the depredations of man as a hunter. It is possible, even likely, that at one time the various Inuit peoples achieved a balanced existence with whales and seals, in much the same way as seals and Polar Bears exist in a fair predator-prey balanced relationship, even though to us this could not be described as 'in harmony'! As the number of men, other than Eskimos, in the Arctic increased, and as the Eskimos themselves adopted the trappings of modern civilization in the form of motorized boats, rifles, and explosive harpoons, so the large sea mammals suffered.

Early explorers found large numbers of whales, which were soon hunted and slaughtered for their whalebone bristles, for oil, and also as an occasional bonus, for ambergris, a strange fatty stomach inclusion invaluable as a basis for the creation of perfumes.

Whaling around Spitzbergen began early in the 1600s, with British, Dutch and Danish whaling crews, soon to be followed by the French, Germans, Spanish and Portuguese. Hunting pressure was such that the principal target, the Greenland Whale, became too scarce for profitable hunting within just thirty years, and the international whaling fleet searched further afield. This led them primarily to Greenland seas, where the sad process of depletion of whale stocks by overhunting was soon repeated. In the early 1700s, the centre of operations shifted to the Davis Strait, and a century or so later was more or less confined to Baffin Bay, to be abandoned early in the 20th century after 300 years of over-exploitation. Hopefully, commercial whaling has now ceased for ever in the Northern

ABOVE: Sadly, some whaling continues in Iceland – a whaling station and the remains of a Sperm Whale.

RIGHT: Narwhal tusks, saved from the kill by Baffin Island Inuit, to be carved later into knives, harpoons and ornaments.

Hemisphere, though kills by Eskimos (*saugs-sats*) still occur, and sadly Iceland continues the needless persecution under the guise of research, albeit on a comparatively small scale.

Initially it was the whalebone that marketed best, latterly the oil derived from the whale blubber. Even in most recent times, whale hunting was a brutal, gory business, involving a level of cruelty impossible to justify in a civilized society. Oil and whalebone could be considered as practically useful natural products, ripe for 'harvesting', but ambergris must be regarded as a cosmetic trapping associated with a highly artificial human life-style. Such an artificial human life-style was also to cause problems for the seals. Immensely practical though sealskin boots, clothes and boats may be to Eskimo tribespeople, the use of seal pup skins to produce elegant fur coats for the ladies living in temperate climates has no such essential purpose. For both groups of animals, the abundance of approachable quarry that the early explorers found in the Arctic waters very speedily dim-

inished to a situation of comparative scarcity, and sometimes even rarity or near-extinction as demand relentlessly exceeded supply, aided by swift advances in hunting and killing technology.

Most Arctic whales are essentially summer visitors, but the Narwhal, the Beluga and the very rare Greenland Whale may be present year-round, usually keeping just to the south of the ice-cap. Occasionally, January winds may split the ice sheet, opening leads that may tempt the whales further north than is sensible for them. If subsequent ice movement traps them in one of these leads, the local Eskimos indulge in a *saugssat*. This almost always involves either Narwhals or Belugas, and as packs of whales fight each other for breathing space, the Eskimos gather round and harpoon as many as they can from the edge of the ice. Often the slaughter is considerable, and results in much instant feasting as well as in the storage of abundant meat to help the Eskimos survive the remainder of the winter.

By March, most Belugas are pressing northwards, females accompanied by young first, the males up to a month later. As they travel, their principal foods are the more common larger fish, Cod, Halibut and Haddock. Narwhal are also moving northwards at this time, feeding on fish as they go, but the Greenland Whale, though also migrating north, fuels its journey with massive quantities of krill, filtered from the sea by the baleen plates in its massive jaw. The Arctic krill is at its greatest density in mid-summer, round about July, and can be so concentrated that the chill waters seem almost as thick as a good fish soup. In the Arctic, 'krill' is more of a collective term than in the Antarctic, where it refers more or less specifically to *Euphausia* shrimps. In the Arctic it is composed of a mixture of pelagic or planktonic small animals and their larval stages (no matter how sedentary the adult, marine invertebrates often have highly mobile pelagic larvae), including a variety of crustaceans besides shrimps, sea-slugs, snails and other molluscs, and a number of worms. Often it is the shrimps that predominate, but in July it may be the Pteropods or sea-slugs that form the bulk. It seems amazing that so small a prey can occur in such seemingly hostile waters at a density sufficient to make feeding easy for a creature so huge as a whale.

During the summer, Beluga may often gather in hundreds, or even thousands, in the shallow sheltered waters of the estuaries feeding into Hudson's Bay. At sites like the mouth of the Churchill River, cloudy with snow melt-water, the local Eskimo may net large numbers each year. Small for a whale, the Beluga is pinkish-white in colour, and remarkably supple when swimming. Their flukes seem much more loosely-jointed than other whales, and they can turn their bulbous heads to an appreciable degree: they can reverse in mid-water, like a monstrous humming bird, by adjusting the swimming angles of their fore-flukes and sculling with them.

They are one of the mainstays of Eskimo economy, and not just because of the occasional *saugssat*. They are relatively easily caught and handled, and produce a nourishing dark meat, best eaten, according to the Eskimo, after a period of natural cold-storage in an ice-covered cache. They also provide one of the better quality oils for lamps, one which burns with a clear white flame whilst giving off considerable warmth. To the Eskimo, they also provide a delicacy called '*mattak*': this is derived from the Beluga skin after a period of maturation in cold storage – equivalent to good hanging in butchery terms – and is considered delectably spicy.

Narwhals, though less favoured in the diet and often moving in quite small 'pods' of five to twenty individuals, may be easier prey to the Eskimo hunter because they stay near the surface for long periods. The males possess a tusk, often a couple of metres in length, with clockwise spiral markings. However unlikely it may seem, this may be one possible origin of the legend of the unicorn so popular in coats of arms and in fable. It is the left upper canine tooth that develops into the tusk, which may play some part in display but rarely seems to have been observed in aggressive use – though often the tusk is broken off. Nor does the tusk seem to be used as an ice-breaking tool, and it seems most likely that a major use may be to prod the Halibut, a favourite food which lives on the ocean floor, and force it up into open water where it can be captured.

The other summer visitor whales to the Arctic are in evidence by June. Most remain in low-Arctic waters, but others will push well north. Grey Whales are conspicuous amongst them, with Caaing (a recent colonist of such northerly seas), Finback, Humpback and the massive Blue. Most often seen is the smaller Pike Whale, not only because it is most numerous but because it often comes close inshore. In the extreme north of the Pacific Ocean, the California Grey Whale occurs in summer, before retreating to winter – almost as a tourist attraction – off the west coast of Mexico. Pressing well to the north are packs of black-and-white Killer Whales, or Orcas, with their prominent, tall, slim dorsal fin. Though only of medium size, these are ferocious predators with a similar pack instinct and mouth full of teeth to the hunting dogs of the African veldt. These terrorize Narwhals,

MAIN PICTURE: The
distinctive slender and
upright dorsal fin of a
killer whale, or Orca.
TOP INSET: Fin Whale.
BOTTOM INSET: The tail
flukes of a sounding
Humpback Whale.

Belugas and seals in particular, but will also tackle the larger species, including the Sperm Whale.

Whales in general tend to be widespread and extremely mobile, with many species breeding in tropical waters and migrating north or south to benefit from the summer's seasonal richness in the polar oceans. The Antarctic whales seem more cosmopolitan than those from the Arctic, though specialities like the Beluga and Narwhal are lacking. In the Antarctic, the bias is towards the baleen whale species, flourishing on the huge supplies of krill. Many are now rare, having been hunted almost to extinction in a pattern of events that followed a century or more behind the sad calendar of the Arctic.

Most striking of Antarctic whales is the Blue Whale, biggest of all the whales, but the second-in-size, the Fin Whale, also occurs here. The Blue Whale travels right down to the margin of the ice and spends the whole summer not far from it, feeding on krill. Scientists calculate that Blue Whale numbers were as low as 1,000–5,000 during the 1950s as a result of whaling pressure, and it is not yet known if numbers are increasing with the

cessation of much of the whaling activity. The probability is that recovery – if it indeed occurs – will be exceedingly slow.

Fin Whales keep further to the north in slightly warmer waters, as do the Southern Right Whales. These favour shallow bays, and their habit of gathering in large groups in such locations made them extremely vulnerable to whalers. In addition, they carry (weight for weight) excellent quantities of oil and very high quality baleen. In combination these desirable attributes led to the near-extinction of the Southern Right Whale by the mid-19th century only now, 150 years later, are there signs of a recovery in numbers.

Similarly affected by whaling because of their predictable coastal migration routes, Humpback Whales too were brought to the verge of extinction, with only an estimated 1,000–3,000 remaining during the 1960s. With the larger whales so scarce as to be not worth hunting, and to an extent protected by International Convention, whaling interest centred during the post-war years on the comparatively small Minke (7 tonnes, 8 metres long) and Sei Whales (20 tonnes, 16 metres long). The Sei rarely ventures much further than

Whale bones litter many
sub-Antarctic beaches.

55°S and is now protected, but the smaller Minke feeds adjacent to the ice and remains the only legal quarry until full whaling constraints are in operation.

Of the toothed whales, the ubiquitous Orca, or Killer Whale, occurs in Antarctica, preying on other whales (even tearing the tongues and chunks of flesh out of Sperm Whales), on seals and on penguins. Other toothed whales include the Southern Bottlenose, which feeds on squid and is often found close to the ice, and the Southern Fourtooth, which is very similar in appearance but about which little is known except the highlight of its unusual dentition – only four teeth instead of the usual dozens. Porpoises and dolphins are strangely almost unheard of in Antarctic waters, and only the Hourglass Dolphin occurs with regularity.

At the other end of the size scale is the 30 tonne Sperm Whale, at 14 or 15 metres the longest as well as the heaviest toothed whale. In the 18th and 19th centuries, huge numbers of Sperm Whales were hunted out of Antarctic waters, but a shifting of commercial interests – and a scarcity of whales – has reduced activity ever since, and hunting finished finally in 1979. The Sperm Whale has a sixteen-month gestation period, compared with eleven or twelve months in even the largest of the baleen whales. As with other whales, mating and conception normally takes place in the tropics about a year after the birth of the last calf – thus at about the time it is weaned. Sperm Whale sociology is better understood than that of the other whales. The social group, called variously a school, herd or pod, is based on a harem structure with at its centre ten to fifteen mature cows (they reach maturity at about ten years old), together with their offspring, both recent and those of several previous years. This group is under the protection and control of a harem master bull, usually the biggest whale. Young males leave or are driven off by the harem master well before they reach maturity and they form all-male groups. As they mature – probably at fifteen to twenty years – individuals break away and live a solitary existence until they can fight for control of a harem when they are about twenty-five years old, displacing an ageing bull.

Although the Bearded Seal may remain in high northern latitudes throughout the year, by far the most numerous and widespread year-round resident in the Arctic is the Ringed Seal. Throughout the winter months it will live below the ice-sheet, and its distribution roughly matches the southward extent of the ice. Obviously to survive in such circumstances, it must have a series of blow-holes where it can surface to breathe, and these are kept open through the winter by the use of the teeth and the nails or the flippers, and also by employing the robust head as a battering ram. Surfacing for air is a much more frequent event for the seals than for most whales, because although seals show many adaptations to their partially marine life, neither structurally nor physiologically are those adaptations anywhere near so sophisticated as in the whales. That said, they have an amazingly well developed ability to hunt and catch fish, and to relocate widely scattered breathing-holes below the ice in the near-total darkness of the Arctic winter.

If suitable patches of open water are available, or if the ice-cap is thin enough, then Ringed Seals may occur even at the North Pole as the ice drifts that way. Particularly in the High Arctic, Ringed Seals may be a staple component of the diet of both the polar Eskimos and Polar Bears. Possibly because of this predation, they are not colonial breeders like so many of their fellows, preferring to breed singly. They dig a small cave in a snow drift on the ice-cap, which serves both as shelter from the harshness of the environment out of the water, and to conceal them from hunting Polar Bears. These snow caves are usually constructed close to a crack in the ice, through which the seal slips silently into the water if danger threatens. Ringed Seal young are produced in March and April, and when new-born are helpless. Though they grow quickly on the extremely rich milk (the fat content may be several times greater than in human milk), they are unable to swim until they are weaned a month or so later. Should a Polar Bear attack during this time, the female escapes, abandoning the youngster to its fate.

During the Arctic summer months, the Ringed Seals spend much of their time hauled out on ice floes, apparently sleeping. This may be because during the winter the blow-hole has to be kept open even when the ice may be three metres thick, which necessitates continuous activity, cutting away fresh ice. The seal is unable to snatch even a few hours sleep, nose close to the blow-hole, in case the nose skin – and vital sensory whiskers – freeze to the ice. Summer, with its additional warmth and plentiful food, possibly allows them to catch up on lost sleep.

The other two widespread seals in Arctic waters are migrants, moving north as summer advances from wintering areas in slightly warmer seas. The Harp Seal has possibly the longest migration: many winter off Newfoundland, to summer in Baffin Bay, about 3,500 kilometres to the north. Harp Seals gather on ice floes out in the Atlantic to give birth to their young between January and March. These gatherings may be huge, and are initially largely composed of pregnant females. The males arrive later, and mating takes place after the pups have been born. Many seals have evolved a process of 'delayed implantation', where the fertilized egg is stored, undeveloped, for some months before being released to implant in the wall of the uterus and begin proper development into a foetus. In this way, not only can birth be at the same, most favourable time each year, but the gathering that takes place can also be used for the social purposes of display and mating, without the timing being upset by a gestation period of only a few months rather than a precise year.

The time of birth is obviously crucial for survival, and nowhere is it more critical than in the harsh conditions of the polar regions. Various strategies have been evolved to cope with this: in the seals, the general rule is to give birth at such a time that the chances of survival for the young are maximized. Though a late winter birth may seem at odds with this, for the few weeks after its birth the pup is dependent solely on its mother's very rich milk – it need not hunt for itself. By the spring it is becoming independent and needing to hunt on its own – but the numbers of fish, or other prey, are increasing, so hunting becomes relatively easy. Were the pup to be born in the comparative warmth of the summer months, and then fed to weaning on its mother's milk, it would reach independence in late summer when fish stocks are dwindling and the climate becoming harsher – no time for an inexperienced animal to prepare itself for the savage winter ahead either in

PAGES 122–123:
Young Ringed Seal.

hunting skills or in accumulating the necessary protective blubber layer.

The other migrant is the Hooded Seal, which is both more scarce and normally does not penetrate quite so far to the north. Most concentrate round the southern shores of Greenland in summer, having bred well out to sea on the ice off Newfoundland and Jan Mayen Island. The Hooded Seal is so called because the male has an area of inflatable skin on its nose: this can be blown up when the seal is excited, or in danger, to a large and (to an enemy or predator) daunting hood.

Hooded Seals are fish eaters, and dive very deeply – below 200 metres – to take particularly Halibut and Haddock. Essentially the four High Arctic seals do not compete for food stocks: each has evolved into a separate way of life – a niche in ecological terms – which allows food resources to be equitably shared, avoiding conflict that could be wasteful if not of life certainly of energy. So while the Hooded Seal dives deep for its fish diet, the Bearded Seal grubs around in muddy shallows for molluscs and the occasional flat fish. The Harp Seal has a diet concentrating on mid-water fish, occasionally supplemented by crustaceans, while the Ringed Seal, in

Steller's Sea-Lions.

much the same zone, has a diet largely composed of krill, augmented from time to time with fish.

In the Northern Pacific Ocean, the Pribilof chain of islands holds huge numbers of Pacific Fur Seals, which migrate south to the coast of California for the winter. These 'fur seals' are more accurately called 'eared seals' or sea-lions: not only do they have a small external ear-flap or pinna, but their limbs differ appreciably from those of the true seals. In the true seals, the front limbs have become simple flippers, while the back ones trail limply for much of the time. Sinuous body movements provide effective swimming propulsion, but 'locomotion' on land is slow and laborious, a matter of humping the considerable weight along with all the elegance of a legless caterpillar! As any visitor to a circus or zoo will know, the sea-lions, and other eared seals, are no less masterly as swimmers, but are far more agile on land. Their flippers, front and rear, have effective articulating joints, and indeed on a beach they can run with surprising speed to chase off an intruder or attack a rival.

Pacific Fur Seals, and Steller's Sea-Lions, only just penetrate into Low Arctic waters. They, in common with other seals carrying both dense fur and a layer of blubber, have problems in coping with the heat of a summer day. They pant, flap their flippers like fans, and will often scoop nearby mud or sand over their bodies to reflect some of the sun's glare, before eventually resorting to a cooling – but

perhaps hazardous – dip in the sea.

Fur and blubber have caused the seals other problems. Though in the Arctic whaling (except for the Eskimo *saugssats*) is largely a thing of the past, sadly the equally bloodthirsty carnage of seal-hunting still persists. Hunting seals for the oil that can be extracted from their blubber has ceased, but despite mounting international pressure, seal pups are still clubbed to death so that humans can adorn themselves in coats made of their pelts. At a few weeks old their fur is at its longest and densest, thus prime for fur coat manufacture. For the Eskimos sealskin garments are ideal – possibly even vital for the polar tribes

Bull Southern Sea-Lion (with an Elephant Seal dozing behind).

Rusting vats, relics of past sealing days when blubber was rendered down into oil.

– but the continuance of this slaughter and trade for the residents of temperate Eurasia and the Americas is quite impossible to support in a supposedly environmentally enlightened age. Even if seal populations have not evidently suffered from continued hunting, or indeed if any reduction in numbers due to hunting has in some way maintained the vigour of seal stocks by preventing squalor and starvation due to overcrowding, culling of this nature can hardly be condoned.

During the midsummer months, with many of the seals on the ice for long periods of time, there is a seal 'harvest' season vital to the polar Eskimo tribes. Today they tend to use a high-velocity rifle with telescopic sight at long range, rather than a harpoon backed by incredible stalking stealth and patience as their ancestors did.

The Antarctic seals do not of course face the specialist hunting pressure of the Eskimo, but they have in the past shared with their northern counterparts the pressures of sealers seeking both oil and skins, and these pressures perhaps have had a more striking impact on the Antarctic scene than they have had in the Arctic. Nor are the southern seal populations preyed on by a predator as ruthlessly efficient as the Polar Bear, but in the sea they share with their northern equivalents the hazards of encounters with packs of Killer Whales. And the Antarctic species must face (when young) a predator that does not occur in the Arctic, one of their own kind, the Leopard Seal.

Of the Antarctic seals – the true seals – the Weddell Seal is the most southerly, as well as the most widespread and the most frequently encountered, because it is usually restricted to solid, permanent ice-sheet area. Weddell Seals spend much of the Antarctic summer in small groups, often hauled out on the ice or rocks, sunning or sleeping, as does the Ringed Seal in the Arctic. The usual group size is a handful of cows with a single bull: as in the Sperm Whale, the young bulls form separate 'clubs' of their own, to emerge and challenge for leadership when mature. They favour rough, broken ice which gives greater shelter from piercing winds, even though this makes their heavyweight, slug-like, humping progress across country even more cumbersome.

The pups are born in September and October: a rude shock as they leave the 37°C of

RIGHT: 'Harvesting' seals – still an Inuit way of life on the Pribilof Islands (W. Wisniewski).

their mother's uterus for air temperatures maybe as low as −20°C! The pups are weaned in six weeks or so, after feverish growth and having doubled their birth-weight of 25 kilogrammes: but they have a long way still to go as adult Weddell Seals may weigh 400 kilogrammes. The pups are able to swim with ease as they enter the water, often for the first time, soon after weaning, and are thought to remain with their mother for perhaps two more months, doubtless learning skills by experience all the time.

As a reflection more of their habitat than their diet (usually composed of fish and krill, often caught at depths down to 200 metres), their teeth grow continuously, a situation more commonly found in herbivores. Though their teeth keep growing, their mouths are often in a very battered state, largely because the Weddell Seal (again like the Ringed Seal) overwinters *under* the ice sheet, and must maintain air-holes for breathing, using its teeth to do so. This is the province of the bull, who will fiercely defend his network of blow-holes against rival males, but will tolerate the presence of a few cows – perhaps his harem. Weddell Seals are amongst the most vocal of seals under water, producing a wide range of wails, groans and trilling clicks, possibly partly for communication, but maybe also as an aid to locating blow-holes in total darkness, and indeed prey too.

fine, cat-like, needle-sharp teeth, and feed on squid as well as fish and krill. Little is known of their daily lives, or of the rate of growth of their pups.

Much the same can be said of the Crab-eater Seal, also living in close association with the pack-ice, but venturing well south on occasion during the summer to the shores of the Antarctic Continent. Crabeater Seals have strangely flattened, lobed teeth, which they use as a baleen whale uses its whale-bone plates, to sieve out krill from mouthfuls of water in summer. In winter, when krill is scarce, fish feature more prominently. They are intermediate in weight between Weddell and Ross Seals, but are much the same length as (but thus appreciably slimmer than) Weddell Seals.

The Crabeater Seal offers something of an Antarctic success story – or at least a surprise. The early explorers found the Crabeater Seal rare, encountering only the occasional young individual offshore, and rarely seeing many on the treacherously unstable pack-ice. Recent aerial surveys, however, have shown the Crabeater Seal to occur in such massive numbers that it is suggested that this may be the world's most numerous seal. For all this, still little is known of its biology, but from

The Ross Seal is appreciably smaller, rarely more than 2 metres long and weighing less than 200 kilogrammes. They are scarcer too, and live mostly on or very close to the pack-ice, often at some distance from the Antarctic mainland itself. They have unusually

Weddell Seals.

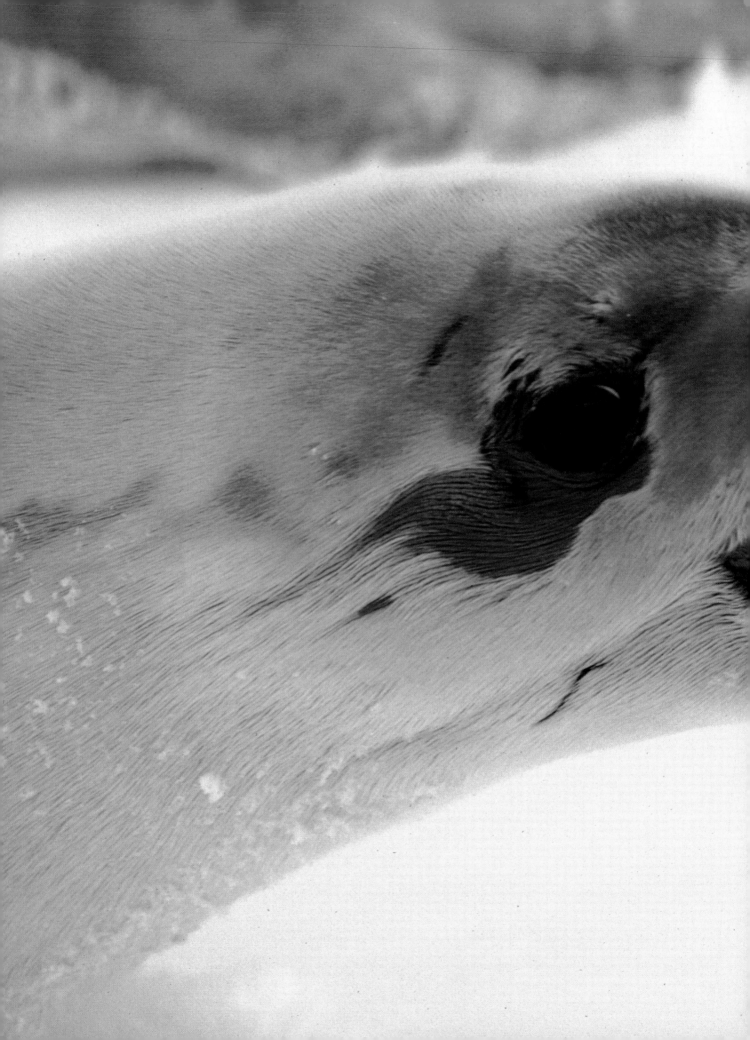

observations of numbers of bull-plus-cow-plus-pup family groups hauled out on the ice in September and October, there is a possibility that Crabeater Seals may be monogamous – a notably unusual event in the world of seals.

The last of the 'true seals' is the Leopard Seal, widespread and often common through both the pack-ice belt and in the open Antarctic ocean. This is a large seal, at three metres or longer and weighing up to 350 kilogrammes. It has a slimmer, more sinuous body than the Weddell Seal, and is noticeably longer and more flexible in the neck, as befits its predatory habits. The name is derived from the large dark spots prominent on the pale background of its underfur. Interestingly, as in predatory birds like falcons, females are detectably (usually about ten per cent) larger than males, though the reason for this (as with much of their biology) is not fully understood.

Leopard Seals have somewhat enigmatic teeth in their large mouths: though their canine teeth are powerfully developed as the fangs of a predator, the molars seem a cross between the carnassial, slicing teeth of a dog and the lobed, krill-collecting molars of the Crabeater Seal. Leopard Seal food *does* include krill during the summer months, but they are essentially predators, snapping up young and inexperienced seal pups in their earliest days in the water, but concentrating especially on a food supply that is present year-round – the small and medium-sized penguins. These they catch, often by lying in wait offshore at regularly used penguin rookery 'landing stages', and with whip-like neck movements, beat the hapless penguin to death, literally turning it inside out to skin it before gulping it down.

The 'eared seals' are represented in the Antarctic by three species, two of them very closely allied fur seals. These are the Kerguelen Fur Seal, which occurs mostly to the north of the Antarctic Convergence and only occasionally south of it, and the Antarctic Fur Seal, which lives on many of the Antarctic Ocean archipelagos south of the Convergence. The Antarctic Fur Seal is called scientifically *Arctocephalus gazella*, the specific epithet *gazella* indicating just how nimble the eared seals can be in clambering around on the rocks.

There are striking size differences between the sexes, but as in most other seals

Crabeater Seal *(C. Carvalho)*.

ABOVE: Leopard Seal hauled out on the Antarctic ice. Usually this large, lithe hunter waits submerged, just off the ice, for unwary penguins to take to the water. LEFT: Largest of the mammals to be found ashore in Antarctica, bull Southern Elephant Seals may tip the scales at four tonnes.

(and in contrast to the Leopard Seal) the bull, at two metres, may be half as long again as the cow, and at 100 kilogrammes, twice her weight. Much of this additional size and weight seems to be in the bulky head and neck, which carries an impressive furry mane. Each bull first sets up as a 'beach-master', patrolling his patch of pebbles or rock some weeks before the cows arrive. He will attract, and vigorously defend, a small harem of perhaps four or five cows, who arrive heavily pregnant and produce pups in November and December. The young weigh only a few kilogrammes at birth, quite tiny compared with other seals, and are clad in dense black fur. They are fed by their mothers for three months or more, appreciably longer than other seals.

The fur of the adults consists of a dense, waterproof and windproof underpelt, often 2 or 3 centimetres thick, protected by an outer layer of longer guard hairs, which help shed water quickly on emerging from the sea. These characteristics are most desirable in furriers' eyes. It is on record that the South Shetlands yielded 320,000 skins in four years early in the 19th century, and ultimately the fur trade in Europe and Asia almost eliminated the Fur Seals. Only now, fortunately, are numbers recovering rapidly to the present estimate of 300,000.

Lastly, the largest and most spectacular of the Antarctic seals is the Southern Elephant Seal. The males are gigantic and grotesque, often reaching 7 metres in length (with a 'waistband' of up to 4 metres!) and a weight of up to 4 tonnes. Females are essentially much more seal-like, and weigh about one tonne, with a length of 3–4 metres. Not that they are otherwise difficult to identify, but the bull has a loose, wrinkled area of skin on the face above the nostrils. This can be inflated at will, and in older males can form quite a substantial elephant-like 'trunk'. This functions as a sounding-box for the bull's aggressive roarings, which continue with deafening and unending regularity for some months from early October.

The world population of the Southern Elephant Seal may now be nearing the one-million mark, an amazing recovery from their over-exploitation as a source of oil during the 19th century. The biggest current colony, over 300,000 strong, is on one of the old sealers' strongholds, South Georgia. All col-

onies tend to be huge, often tens of thousands strong, unbelievably noisy and smelly, with Elephant Seals packed side by side on suitable beaches. The bulls arrive first, and set up territories on beaches throughout the sub-Antarctic, to be joined within a few weeks by the already-pregnant cows.

The normal harem is about twenty or thirty cows, and their defence must be fierce, as marauding immature males are always on the lookout at the fringes of the colony to found their own dynasty. Battles between rival bulls are often ferocious, bloody and long-drawn-out. The opponents rear up, then crash together with bone-jarring body-checks, teeth at the ready, lunging at each others necks. The blood is often only superficial, but continuous fighting weakens both victor and vanquished. Such territorial skirmishes continue after the pups are born, and despite their substantial size (one metre long, 50 kilogrammes in weight) the pups run the risk of serious injury by being trampled.

Pups are fed frequently for three weeks on milk with a fat content perhaps eight times that of human milk, by which time they have quadrupled their birth weight and almost doubled in length. Within days they will put to sea, the cows will mate with the harem master, and then they too will return to the marine environment to replenish depleted fat stocks before winter. A wide variety of squid, crustaceans and fish feature in the Elephant Seal diet, and recent evidence indicates that they may dive to 3,000 metres in search of food: as deep or deeper than any whale.

The Southern Fur Seal was hunted almost to extinction for its fur, but is making a rapid comeback now hunting has ceased.

8

BIRDS

If called upon to nominate *the* family of birds typifying polar regions, most people would surely name the penguins. Certainly, they do show extreme adaptations to a marine life, but though we associate them so strongly with the Antarctic, of the twenty-one world species only eight breed within the area here defined as Antarctica, and only two on the Antarctic Continent itself. The remainder occupy the cool-temperate belt of Southern Hemisphere oceans.

Most authorities consider that forty-three species of birds breed in Antarctica, of which the vast majority can in one way or another be classified as seabirds. These are by nature better insulated with a denser plumage than most land birds, and tend to be both larger (in general) and certainly better at flying in the extremely stormy conditions often prevalent in southern oceans. These adaptations to survival in cool marine environments were developed aeons before the polar regions existed: with the evolution of the polar ice-caps, most habitable terrestrial environments disappeared, leaving the various seabirds in undisputed control of the few small dry land areas that remained.

Although the Antarctic landscape is barren and the climate severe in the extreme, the surrounding oceans (despite being stormy) are both appreciably warmer and teeming with food: fish, squid, and the assemblage of small to microscopic animal life called plankton. Most of the Antarctic birds depend on this rich food source for at least half the year. Although the majority of Antarctic birds breed on the windswept rocky islands on the northern fringes of Antarctica, protected as often as not by expanses of Tussock Grass, nineteen species breed in the pack-ice zone or on the Antarctic mainland itself. These include five penguins and eight petrels, a handful of terns, commorants and a skua, and one land bird – the only one – the strange scavenging Sheathbill, ubiquitous along shorelines, around seabird and seal colonies, and around the various scientific bases.

Further to the north, beyond the Antarctic Convergence where cold waters from the Antarctic Ocean meet the warmer seas of the South Atlantic and South Pacific Oceans, not only are sea temperatures higher but the climates of the islands, though often wet and windy, are still much more benign than in Antarctica itself. Grasses and other herbaceous plants flourish, though the number of plant species may not be great, and there are shrubs and occasionally even windswept trees to provide a more varied habitat. Often, though, these habitats are under-used and seabirds still dominate, such is the isolation of the islands from major continental sources of land bird colonists. In the sector to the south of Australasia land bird variety is strengthened by the arrival of birds as diverse as parrots, the Starling and various thrushes from Australia, while on the Falkland Islands, comparatively favourably situated adjacent to the

PAGES 132–133:
An Adélie Penguin in characteristically cautious pose before diving in.

Striated Caracara.

southern tip of South America, something like two-thirds of the resident breeding birds can be fairly classed as land birds.

Compared with the area south of the Antarctic Convergence with its forty-three species, the Falkland Islands themselves have a list of around 175 regularly-occurring birds, with perhaps another fifty species on record as occasional vagrants from South America. Of these, some sixty-six species breed regularly, fifteen of them as island-endemic subspecies, that is distinctive sub-species or races breeding only on the Falk-lands. Five species of penguin and no less than twenty-eight petrels, of all sizes, maintain the links with Antarctica, while many of the waders and gulls would be familiar to a visiting American ornithologist. South American specialities are represented by such birds as the Striated and Crested Caracaras, but even a birdwatcher from the temperate zones of the Northern Hemisphere would find the Barn Owl, Short-eared Owl, and the Swallow (or Barn Swallow in North America) readily identifiable. Confronted with such 'homely' birds in such remote places, the zoological distribution term 'cosmopolitan' takes on its true meaning.

But returning to the Antarctic proper, it is suitable to begin not with the penguin family but with those birds most numerous there in terms of both numbers of species and numbers of individuals (and thus perhaps more properly regarded as 'typical'), the petrels. Voyaging southwards from the Equator, the traveller passes across a broad band of ornithologically uninteresting ocean (be it Pacific, Atlantic or Indian). As much as by the lack of passing birds, this tropical belt is indicated by the 'beautiful blue' of the seas. Once it is left behind, not just the stormy winds of the 'Roaring Forties' and 'Furious Fifties' latitudes, but more the slightly milky green tinge to the sea, which is indicative of massive planktonic growth (occasionally with krill and other zooplankton, and with some marine algae, the tinge may be reddish), herald the richness of the seabird life around, for this plankton is the basis of their food chains.

Largest of all the petrels are the alba-trosses. In common with others of their family, they have beaks in which the junctions of the various horny plates that compose the beak's outer sheath can be clearly seen, and on the

Tussock-Bird – *the* small bird of the sub-Antarctic.

ridge of the beak all possess paired, tubular nostrils. These are perhaps least developed in the albatrosses and most evident in some of the smallest storm petrels. Their function is hotly debated: some argue that they are the external evidence of a sense of smell far better developed than in other birds. There are various anatomical aspects of the internal convoluted plate structure of the nostril, and of the brain, that would support such a view, and indeed many of the petrels do smell powerfully, even to the comparatively poorly developed human nose. It may even be that, returning to their enormous colony – after dark for safety – some petrels use the individually distinctive smell of their mate to locate the nest, an otherwise difficult task. The other school of thought sees the tubular nostrils as a form of air-speed indicator of the Pitot-tube type (familiar as the long slim tube protruding from the nose or wingtips of modern jet aircraft). As many of the petrels (and certainly not least the albatrosses) are masters of energy-economic flight, using every upcurrent available off the waves, an accurate speed sensor would seem invaluable, and we have no knowledge of any other organ serving this purpose.

The albatrosses of the Antarctic breed on the windswept Tussock Grass on the islands just north of the pack-ice: none breed on the Continent itself. South Georgia and the Iles Kerguelen hold four species: Black-browed (occasionally occurring with Gannets in the

Northern Hemisphere), Grey-headed, Light-mantled Sooty and Wandering. All fly not just with effortless ease, but with a characteristic master pattern. The albatross will steadily build up speed, with wings held in an 'M' to reduce drag and increase rapidity, but with little or no wing movements, in a long shallow dive with the wind on its flank or almost behind it. As it nears the surface, it will turn along a wave trough and then use its accumulated speed, and the upcurrent of air off the crest of the swell, to gain height quickly (perhaps climbing to 20 metres above the waves) with no wingbeats but with wings at full stretch for maximum lift, before again turning and setting off on a renewed 'downhill' glide, picking up speed as it loses height. In this way, albatrosses can travel far and fast, out of the breeding season, circumnavigating the globe as a routine in the windiest latitudes of 40° and 50° S.

All albatrosses are characterized by extremely long, slender wings, often held rigidly at right-angles to the body. The Wandering Albatross has the greatest wingspan of any seabird at 3 metres or more, and may weigh around 10 kilogrammes. The other Antarctic species are smaller, at 2 metres or more wingspan and weighing only 3 or 4 kilogrammes.

Albatrosses have large eyes – indicating a well-developed power of sight – and scan the sea as they fly for concentrations of food. Once this is located, the bird settles and with its huge, hooked beak gobbles (this is the appropriate word for it) as much fish, or squid, or large zooplankton as it can – often to the extent that take-off (already a complicated manoeuvre because of the length of the wings) may be impeded further by the sheer weight of prey. If they are not involved in feeding young, digestion takes place routinely, but if they are, the food is rendered down into a tacky, oily mixture which is regurgitated to the youngster when the adult returns – maybe hours but often days later. Both adults and young use this pungent oil in defence, being able to eject it with reasonable accuracy over a couple of metres range. So offensive, and sticky, is it that even aggres-

Masterly energy conservation: Black-browed Albatross in flight.

Few nest-sites could have a better view: Black-browed Albatross.

sive predators like the Great Skua may be repelled, or even immobilized if the feathers get saturated.

The three smaller albatrosses breed in colonies, often in flattish areas on the islands, and often in enormous numbers, usually amongst the Tussock Grass. They make volcano-shaped, untidy nests about 30 centimetres high and almost one metre in diameter, and lay a single, rather large egg. The Wandering Albatross, which is often a solitary breeder, lays in mid-November, and then the sexes brood the egg in turns lasting several days for around eighty days before it hatches. The youngster, despite its rich food and effective protection from the cold in terms of thick down and an insulating fatty or blubber layer, may remain in the nest for almost a year before fledging. Visits from food-bearing parents, after the first few weeks when one or other is constantly in attendance to ward off any attack from Great Skuas, occur at several-day intervals, as the parents may hunt far out to sea. There is one recovery of a ringed bird, with a nestling to feed, from the coast of Australia, almost 4,000 kilometres away from its nesting island, indicative of the vast distances that albatrosses may travel as a routine.

In consequence, the annual breeding cycle so familiar in most birds is unattainable, and successful breeders miss a year, staying out at sea and getting back into good condition. It may be several years before the fledgeling returns, and two or three years after that before it settles on a mate and begins to breed. Courtship display is elaborate: the pair dance cumbersomely face to face, often with wings outstretched, and preen each others necks, all of this accompanied by a weird variety of groans and much beak snapping, which makes a fearsome noise.

The Giant Petrel or Giant Fulmar – which occurs in two forms, Northern and Southern – is almost the size of the smaller albatrosses. This is the voracious scavenger of the Antarctic, setting about any carrion (such as a dead seal or whale) with disgusting and gory enthusiasm, emerging often from within the carcass smeared with the remains and sometimes too bloated to fly. Not content merely with scavenging, Giant Petrels patrol penguin

Giant Petrels in a typical
fight over food.

colonies in particular, and are quick to take advantage of an unguarded egg or defenceless or injured chick, quickly despatching their victim with the powerfully hooked tip of their beak. Egg incubation lasts for eight or nine weeks (roughly similar to the smaller albatrosses) and the chicks stay in the nest for another four months (in contrast to the seven months taken by the smaller albatrosses to fledge). These are strongly- and heavily-built birds, with stiff wings and a characteristic flight with spells of wingbeats interspersed with prolonged glides.

Of the medium-sized petrels, the Antarctic Fulmar (quite similar to its Northern Hemisphere relative) and the Antarctic and Snow Petrels all breed at suitable sites on the Antarctic Continent and Peninsula, as well as on the islands north of the pack-ice. The blotchy brown and white Antarctic Petrel breeds in huge colonies – some estimated at one million or more birds strong – and flies with a series of stiff-winged glides between wingbeats, hovering (often some metres above the waves) before diving shallowly

for prey. The Snow Petrel is the only all-white small petrel in the world, and is usually confined to the pack-ice belt and the seas close to it. It has an erratic flight, like a long-winged, ghostly-white bat, jinking between ice floes as it dips to the surface to snatch plankton to feed.

It is the great flocks of smaller petrels, always on the move, often following vessels, that so typify Antarctic and sub-Antarctic waters. Most of these will be breeding in enormous colonies on the Antarctic Islands, usually amongst the rocks in screes or in burrows beneath the roots of Tussock Grass clumps. Wilson's Petrel is one leading contender for the title of the world's commonest seabird. Almost all are nocturnal in their habits, a protection evolved (as is burrow nesting) to reduce the levels of predation, particularly at the hands of the Great Skua and others of similar ilk. At sea various members of the petrel family often feed in loose association with each other – each benefiting from the food-finding capability of the others, though not in direct competition for precisely

the same food items. This provides an excellent example of the partitioning of the food resources of an outwardly rather uniform habitat.

The shearwaters (named for their habit, when gliding, of cutting the surface of the water with one wing-tip), here represented by the Grey Petrel and White-chinned Petrel, float buoyantly on the surface and dabble for small squid and krill, only occasionally diving to catch food just below the surface. The smallest of the petrels – thrush-sized birds like the Black-bellied Storm Petrel and Wilson's Petrel – flutter moth-like just above the surface, often (and characteristically in the case of Wilson's) dabbling their feet on the surface before dipping down to take tiny fish and crustaceans. The larger gadfly petrels – the Kerguelen Petrel, Blue Petrel and White-headed Petrel, for example, take appreciably

LEFT: Snow Petrel
(C. Carvalho).
BELOW: Antarctic Petrel:
two of the smaller
members of the petrel
family that dominates
Antarctic bird life.

larger prey, also by dipping down to the surface in flight, rarely landing, but have appreciably more robust beaks than the storm petrels. Diving petrels, as their name implies, fly low, and catch their prey in shallow dives from the air – the South Georgia and Kerguelen Petrels for example. Last in this array are the three species of prions, the Dove Prion, Fulmar Prion and Thin-billed Prion. Each of these flutters elegantly over the waves, dabbling for small zooplanktonic animals, and it is thought that competition is

PAGES 140–141: Wilson's
Petrel 'walking' on a
mirror-calm Antarctic
Ocean – typical of this
species when feeding.

Fairy Prion: the tubular nostrils of the petrel family are particularly evident.

avoided by subtle differences in the fine filter-feeding mechanism that forms part of their complex beaks, which more than anything resemble miniaturized versions of the whalebone plates of the baleen whales.

Although only two species of penguin breed on the Antarctic Continent proper, these are representative of the others breeding only slightly further to the north. Each has a startling life cycle, overcoming hazards of epic proportions. All penguins share an anatomy greatly modified from the basic avian pattern, modified particularly to serve them in a largely marine environment rather than necessarily a polar one, though this function, too, is served by secondary adaptations. First and foremost amongst these structural modifications is the penguin's shape: so well streamlined is it for underwater high-speed swimming that in outline (slightly broader around the 'shoulder' area than the 'hips', with a pointed beak and small head connected to the shoulders by a very short neck) it closely resembles a modern torpedo – or, more appropriately, many of the porpoises and dolphins. In fact, many penguins adopt porpoise tactics when swimming, taking a switchback path through the water often at such a speed that they break the surface and travel some metres through the air, at speeds which may exceed 25 kph.

Next in order of adaptation is the loss of flight. Most authorities consider, on the evidence of their skeleton, that the penguins way back in geological time descended from birds that could fly; but the fossil record of intermediate stages is unclear, and tells us only that many millions of years ago the

penguins stood man-size at two metres high! Though the power of flight has been lost, the wings themselves remain, complete with, if anything, enhanced muscular power. As in the porpoises, the bony skeleton is shortened and flattened to produce an oar-blade-like flipper; the feathers, too, are compressed almost to scales to improve water flow over the penguin's main organs of propulsion. The body feathers, also, are much modified: a dense and extremely effective insulating layer of down is sheathed in hard, flattened and heavily oiled feathers looking not in the least like those of a land bird. These overlap rather like the tiles on a roof, and are lubricated with a greasy substance from the preen gland situated near the penguin's tail, both features combining to make an effective waterproof protection for the down beneath. Emerging regularly from very rough seas on to rock or ice shelves is a physically demanding process: structurally, penguins are adapted to take the knocks by possessing tough feathers, and indeed a tough but flexible leathery skin. Beneath the skin is a layer of blubber which serves the double purpose of shock-absorbing when the penguin jumps or is thrown by the surf on to the shore, and insulation, not just in the icy seas but much more important, whilst the penguin is on land with temperatures at −50°C or lower, exacerbated by an extreme wind-chill factor.

The Emperor Penguin is the largest of the modern penguins, standing 1.5 metres high. In all probability this is not just the most Antarctic of all birds, but the most polar of birds. It breeds in huge numbers in about twenty colonies (or 'rookeries') scattered in sheltered bays around the coast of the Antarctic Continent itself, and on sea ice and rocky islands nearby. It was Dumont d'Urville, in the *Astrolabe*, who found the first Emperor Penguin egg in Adélie Land in 1839, but the British explorer James Clark Ross spotted the first adults to be seen and recorded in detail by man on his 1842 expedition.

The Emperor Penguin retained this association with the south polar explorers when Scott's 1911 expedition sent a team from Cape Evans to Cape Crozier to obtain some eggs for scientific investigation. Apsley Cherry Garrard, leader of the team, graphically described their nightmare journey in the depths of winter as 'the worst journey in the world' – a phrase that will remain always in the annals of polar exploration. Part of the account certainly bears quotation:

'We saw the emperors standing all together huddled under the Barrier cliff some hundreds of yards away. The little light was going fast: we were much more excited about the approach of complete darkness and the look of wind in the south than we were about our triumph. After indescribable effort and hardship we were witnessing a marvel of the natural world, and we were the first and only men who had ever done so: we had within our grasp material which might prove of the utmost importance to science: we were turning theories into facts with every observation we made – and we had but a moment to give.

The disturbed emperors made a tremendous row, trumpeting with their curious metallic voices. There was no doubt they had eggs, for they tried to shuffle along the ground without losing them off their feet. But when they were hustled, a good many eggs were dropped and left lying on the ice, and some of these were quickly picked up by the eggless emperors who had probably been waiting a long time for the opportunity.'

Two major factors dominate the Emperor Penguin breeding season: the fact that the juvenile should reach independence of its parents as the ice melts, so that food is close at hand, and the need for the rookery location to remain frozen throughout incubation. As soon as the sea ice begins to form at the start of the Antarctic winter, Emperor Penguins head for their rookeries, which may be 100 kilometres away from the coast. This journey is of course made on foot, with only occasional relief when they are able to lie belly-down on ice slopes, and using their flippers to help, toboggan along. After reaching the colony the female (still in good condition after a summer of rich feeding on the abundance of Antarctic seafood) lays her single large egg, and almost immediately passes it to the care of the male. Quickly he places it on top of his feet, and drops over it a tea-cosy-like flap of skin, rich in blood vessels, which provides the body-heat necessary for incubation. As the egg is passed from one parent to the other, they both raise their heads in a brief display, producing a trumpeting, donkey-like call.

The female then sets off back across the ice to the sea, there to feed voraciously, diving to depths of 300 metres and more, to build up

Emperor Penguins, still covered in the dense, fluffy down of youth, huddled together against the biting Antarctic wind (*C. Carvalho*).

A group of mature
King Penguins.
(Stephen Leatherwood).

her body-weight again. For the next sixty days or so, the male retains the egg, not daring to expose it even briefly to the savagery of the Antarctic midwinter. Temperatures may drop to −40°C, blizzards may occur, but the embryo must not be exposed to a fatal chill. During this ordeal, all he can do is to stand, back into the wind, and at the most extreme times huddle together with his colleagues in the rookery to conserve warmth. There is little movement to be seen – movement would waste precious energy. Over the incubation period his blubber layer (in good thick condition on arrival) will shrink markedly and he may lose about one third of his body-weight.

When the egg is due to hatch, with impeccable timing the females return from the sea, well fattened and carrying a crop full of fish. This they feed to the newly-hatched nestling, while the emaciated male sets off for the sea to recover and to collect the next batch of fish and krill as food. By now, in early spring, the fish stocks are building up fast so fishing is comparatively easy for the adults, who take it

in turns to guard the youngster or go fishing. The chicks are covered in dense down, and are closely guarded by their parents against Great Skua and Giant Petrel attacks for about six weeks, after which, large enough to look after themselves, they gather in large crèches while both parents devote all their time to fishing in order to feed their fast-growing youngster. The young leave the rookery in mid-summer, about six months after the breeding cycle began, but they reach the sea at the time that the climate is mildest and food is available in plenty, enhancing their chances of survival.

The saga is not yet over for the adults. As all other birds, they must change their worn feathers in the process known as moult. Although they do not have to face the hazards of becoming suddenly flightless, which some larger birds like ducks and geese do, they *must* moult quickly. When appreciable areas of feathers are shed, they lose insulation, and more important waterproofing. Thus they cannot swim or hunt in case they become waterlogged or freeze in a sudden autumnal cold

spell. The Emperors carry out their moult drifting slowly north on ice floes, but soon they are back in the sea and getting into condition for the overland trek back to the rookery again.

The Adélie Penguin, standing at 75–80 centimetres, is typical of the medium-sized penguins in stature, but extraordinary in that it shares with the Emperor the ability to survive on the Antarctic Continent. The most southerly known Adélie rookery is at Cape Royds, less than 1,500 kilometres from the South Pole, and Adélies show amazing navigational skills in finding such remote spots as the Hope Bay rookery, a march of over 350 kilometres from the sea.

Commonest and most widespread of the penguins in the Antarctic, the Adélie spends much of the winter well out to sea off the pack-ice. In September and October, the Antarctic spring, they begin the return journey to their colony. In all probability this will be the colony in which they were born and mated, because most show a very strong fidelity to their mate, despite the fact that

during the winter the pair have probably been far apart. There is mounting evidence that faithfulness to the same mate, the same colony and indeed the same nest-site, year by year, is reflected in the increased breeding success.

The journey from the sea to the colony is on foot – at 'speeds' as slow as 5 kph – with occasional bursts of belly-tobogganing down suitable slopes. Often the nest-site is still snow-covered on their return, but with unerring accuracy the pair meet up at the right spot. Navigation is very much the Adélies' strong point, and experiments have shown that they can 'home' from anywhere on the ice, given that the weather is clear. In overcast conditions they wander aimlessly, but under clear skies, or intermittent cloud, they have an excellent sense of sun angle and of time (to allow for the traverse of the sun across the sky), and are able to 'home' on their colony with great precision.

Adélie Penguins have an elaborate greeting and courtship display, particularly

ABOVE: An Adélie Penguin rookery on King George Island.

BELOW: Chinstrap Penguin.

prominent when the pair have just been re-united at the nest-site. Head and neck are stretched upwards, while the wings beat slowly and from the open beak comes a drumming call. The head feathers are then raised in a crest, the beak closed and a raucous braying call produced. In the so-called 'ecstatic display', the pair stand breast to breast, beaks almost touching, braying loudly, and this serves as the pattern for the 'greeting ceremony' whenever an absent male returns to the nest. In addition, the male will present the female with pebbles, and with these she will build a shallow nest into which she lays two eggs. Display, nest-building and egg-laying are closely synchronized through-out even a massive rookery (some are esti-mated to hold a million or more birds).

The male carries the major burden of incubation while the female returns to the sea. His weight may fall from 6 down to 4 kilo-grammes. Hatching occurs after about six weeks, then both parents share feeding duties alternately, until the young are about a month old, when they gather into crèches, leaving both parents free to collect food – necessary as their appetites are huge. The crèches offer considerable protection from the elements, as the weather can be fickle and summer blizzards are by no means rare. The youngsters huddle together to gain as much protection and benefit from their col-lective warmth as possible, relying on their fat deposits and thick down – and the out-turned protective backs of those unfortunate enough to be on the edge of the group – to keep out the cold. Once in crèches, it is up to the young

RIGHT: **Adélie Penguins** tobogganing. FAR RIGHT: **Gentoo Penguin.** BELOW RIGHT: **Rockhopper Penguin.**

Magellanic Penguin – a burrow-nesting species.

to look after themselves: their parents return regularly with food (and despite the huge mob of apparently identical young, will only feed their own offspring) but will do little or nothing to fend off an attack from a Great Skua or from a Sheathbill.

The greatest hazard faced by the Adélie Penguin, young or old, is the Leopard Seal, an astute and ferocious predator often lying in wait, nostrils and eyes only showing above the water, close beside a favourite Adélie landing shelf. Perhaps because of this, Adélie Penguins always seem hesitant to enter the water singly. Often a group will gather, and not until the pressure from behind becomes irresistible, toppling the front row into the surf, will the rest follow in a black-and-white torrent. On their return, they often make use of their underwater speed to shoot out of the water, like miniature Polaris missiles fired by a submarine, describing a graceful arc through the air before landing. As penguins are not the most nimble of birds on their feet, and as the landing is often extremely slippery, unseemly head-over-heels tumbles are not uncommon.

Further to the north, but still within the

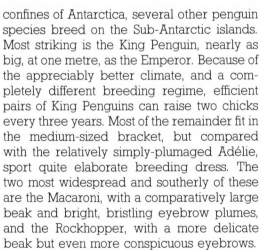

confines of Antarctica, several other penguin species breed on the Sub-Antarctic islands. Most striking is the King Penguin, nearly as big, at one metre, as the Emperor. Because of the appreciably better climate, and a completely different breeding regime, efficient pairs of King Penguins can raise two chicks every three years. Most of the remainder fit in the medium-sized bracket, but compared with the relatively simply-plumaged Adélie, sport quite elaborate breeding dress. The two most widespread and southerly of these are the Macaroni, with a comparatively large beak and bright, bristling eyebrow plumes, and the Rockhopper, with a more delicate beak but even more conspicuous eyebrows.

Of the other shore birds in the Antarctic, the largest and most colourful are two species of cormorant, which fish in shallow waters close to sheltered coasts. These are the Blue-eyed Cormorant, which breeds as far south as the Antarctic Peninsula and on a number of Antarctic and Sub-Antarctic islands, and the Kerguelen Cormorant, widely distributed north of the Convergence but found only on Kerguelen Island south of it. Both species, like their counterparts in more temperate seas,

Still partly clad in its warm nestling down, an immature King Penguin prepares for the Antarctic.

nest on sheltered ledges or beneath boulders, in small colonies, the nest itself being a pile of kelp glued together with guano. The young of many birds show clear signs of their long-distant reptilian ancestry, and none more so than the cormorants, whose grotesquely ugly chicks call to mind artist's impressions of the pterodactyls!

Only one gull, the massive jet-black and white Dominican Gull nests in the Antarctic proper, again as far south as the Antarctic Peninsula and on most of the off-lying islands. They are solitary birds, resident year-round and surviving well on a mixture of scavenging on carrion, predation on other bird's eggs and young, and on their excellent fishing capability. Two tern species breed far south. The

Antarctic Tern, very much the ecological equivalent of the Arctic Tern, comes into Antarctic waters as a migrant in summer to breed, but has nowhere near so spectacular a migratory journey as the Arctic Tern and winters only a short distance to the north of the pack ice. The other, the Kerguelen Tern, is resident year-round near Kerguelen and other islands at similar or more northerly latitudes. Both feed, as do their Northern Hemisphere relatives, by plunge-diving only shallowly from flight to catch small fish and other planktonic animals.

Related to the gulls are the Antarctic's Great Skuas. Alert birds, they are always first overhead when humans set foot on the Antarctic mainland or islands. Huge, gull-

Close-packed, raised conical nests typify a King Shag colony, but the picture cannot convey the accompanying smell and noise.

shaped, but speckled dark brown in plumage, they draw attention with the broad white patches visible on their wings in flight, and with their dog-like barking calls. It is now generally accepted that there are two species: the Antarctic Skua which breeds on the South American coast, on the Falkland Islands, on many islands in the Sub-Antarctic, and on the extreme northerly tip of the Antarctic Peninsula; and the South Polar or McCormick's Skua. This occurs in two colour phases: a paler-plumaged type in more southerly breeding grounds, and a dark form further north on the Antarctic Peninsula. Most of the South Polar Skua breeding colonies are on the fringes of mainland Antarctica itself. While the Antarctic Skua is largely confined to its breeding areas year-round, the South Polar Skua ranges widely over Southern Hemisphere oceans and is thought to penetrate north of the Equator, particularly in the Pacific, as a regular feature of its non-breeding migratory journeying.

These skuas are aggressive birds – in defence of their territories, they will 'dive-bomb' and often make physical contact with human intruders, a scaring and obviously effective process, especially if both birds of

the pair attack in sequence from different angles! They are also effective opportunist predators, and do take an appreciable toll of the eggs and the young of other Antarctic birds, including penguins. They will spend much time loitering close to a colony, and if an egg or young chick is left uncovered for more than seconds as its parent indulges in a squabble over living space with a neighbour, the skua will dash in and seize a meal.

The other main Antarctic predatory birds are the sheathbills. There are only two species in the world. One, the Black-billed Sheathbill, occurs in the eastern sector of the Sub-Antarctic, breeding on the island groups and tending to develop a separate sub-species for each group. The other is the Yellow-billed Sheathbill, occurring on islands in the western sector and on the coast of the Antarctic Peninsula, and migrating north in winter to Patagonia and the Falkland Islands. The sheathbills are a strange family, and one that zoological taxonomists have found difficult to place. Pigeon-sized and pigeon-like in appearance, their all-white plumage is relieved only by the leathery patches of skin on their faces. The name sheathbill comes from the horny sheath protecting the nostrils at the base of the upper mandible. Their legs are greyish and relatively robust: in fact they spend much of their time running around on the shore, or amongst seal or seabird colonies, on feet that also look quite like those of a pigeon: the Falkland Islanders call them 'kelp pigeons'.

It seems most likely that the sheathbills may be a 'missing link' between the gulls and the waders, as their skeleton shows some likenesses to those of skuas and some to that of the Oystercatcher! They are extremely inquisitive birds, and several of them may follow a scientific worker as he goes around his experiments or meteorological equipment. They are also ardent scavengers, omnivorous, with marked seasonal differences in their diet. In winter they forage along the shoreline for dead fish and krill, and can take limpets off the rocks very neatly, holding the shell in one foot while they eat the mollusc within. During the summer they spend most of their time in and around seal colonies and penguin rookeries. Here again their diet is very varied, ranging from seal dung to morsels of Elephant Seal flesh snipped off (their beaks are sharp) from the edges of

Antarctic Skuas move in with lightning speed on an unguarded Rockhopper Penguin egg.

wounds made during the seal's territorial fights. More often, they get their food from gleaning krill dropped by penguins feeding their young. They have also developed the technique of clambering on to the back of the penguin chick (which is so anxious for its meal that it seems not to notice) and upsetting its balance so that even more krill or fish is dropped – and quickly snapped up by the sheathbills. Untended eggs, weak and help-less small young, and any injured birds also quickly fall victim to their rapacious appetites.

This is a cross-section of Antarctic birdlife, heavily dominated by birds whose real home is the sea, and which come ashore because of the necessity to lay their egg or eggs on dry land. All are masters of the marine environ-ment – the penguins swimming in it, the albatrosses flying effortlessly in the air-currents over it. Though the number of species is comparatively few at forty-three, their adaptations to survival in Antarctic cir-cumstances are fascinating in the extreme, as are the ways in which they partition the rich food resources of their oceanic home.

The most immediate contrast apparent when looking at the birds of the Arctic is the number of species involved. Because of the way that the tundra border of the Arctic merges irregularly and often imperceptibly with birch scrub or boreal forest, reaching a definite total is quite difficult, but the forty-three species of the Antarctic are certainly matched by an equal number of breeding waders alone in the Arctic. To suggest a grand total of the order of 120 species probably errs on the side of conservatism.

The range of birds involved is great: there are several small seed-eating members of the vast Perching Bird assemblage – the Passerines – and also several predominantly insect-eating ones, which though they may arrive later than the seed-eaters in the Arctic (because their food supply is not 'available' until later in the season) in the form of the Wheatear, penetrate just as far north. Seabirds, ducks and waders cover the middle ground when it comes to size, while at the larger end of the scale are Cranes, swans, the Snowy Owl and the Rough-legged Buzzard. The last two, as genuine birds of prey, again present a contrast to the Antarctic, where owls and raptors are absent until the latitude of the Falkland Islands is reached. In the Arctic there are no bird families that are immediately associated in the mind with polar habitats, in the way that the penguins (and to a lesser extent the albatrosses) inevitably are. But as we have seen, even in both these families, despite their fantastic adaptations that allow them to survive so well in Antarctica, the majority of the species are located in much more temperate climates, so this 'speciality' may be more apparent than real. In the Arctic, it is more the individual and often subtle adaptations to survival that catch the eye, rather than the spectacular family characteristics so plain in the albatrosses and penguins.

Other contrasts are apparent: in the Arctic there are very few residents – the Ptarmigan, Raven and Redpoll as land birds, Ross's Gull, Ivory Gull and perhaps also Brunnich's Guillemot and Little Auk as seabirds – which can endure the rigours of the true Arctic climate year-round. The remainder, and obviously the vast majority, are migrants. Here too, there is a contrast. In the Antarctic for many of the birds 'migration' is a matter of a relatively short movement northwards to rather better weather and richer feeding. Even exceptions to this general statement, the albatrosses for example, though travelling phenomenal distances, do so in a circumpolar belt, rather than in the normal broadly north-south orientation of migration pathways.

In the Arctic the groups of birds best represented fall into three categories. The first, the waders or shore birds, have already been mentioned. The other two are the wildfowl – the ducks, geese and swans – with more than twenty species, and that broad group the seabirds – embracing the auks, gulls, terns, skuas and petrels – with about thirty. The great majority of all three of these groups are renowned for their migratory capability. The power of flight confers on birds, more than any other group of animals, the ability to exploit the relatively short-term food abundance occurring seasonally in some habitats which for the rest of the year are uninhabitable because of the severity of the climate. The Arctic region, composed as it is of a great deal of tundra, immensely rich in insect (and small mammal) life during the summer, is an ideal and very worthwhile target for migrant birds. The massive numbers and wide variety of summer visitors breeding in the Arctic testifies quite strikingly to this.

Many of the seabirds, generally in parallel to the state of affairs in the Antarctic, do not travel extreme distances south – though there are exceptions. The waders and ducks as a rule perform long and complex migrations – the waders particularly. Many Arctic breeding waders winter in South America, South Africa, India or Australasia. Long wings and powerful muscles, superb navigational capability and above all an age-old, well-established pattern of migratory routes allows them to do this. Many have regular wintering areas in the Southern Hemisphere, and equally regular 'staging posts' in temperate regions north of the Equator. These may be large inland lakes and marshes, or sheltered coastal bays and estuaries, but their common factor is a great richness in invertebrate food animals – worms, molluscs and small crustaceans like shrimps – on which the migrants in transit feed.

Such feeding areas are vital in that they allow the waders concerned to put on weight, as stored fat, quickly. This additional fat may

LEFT: **Raven with chicks.**

Little Whimbrel
(T. and P. Gardner).

familiar in temperate regions, particularly the sandpipers, stints and shanks. Others may have tiny and indeed little-known breeding populations, birds like the Bristle-thighed Curlew, or the Little Whimbrel and extraordinary Spoon-billed Sandpiper, whose populations may only be a few hundred birds. It is these that are particularly vulnerable to accidental extinction, as much from unforeseen industrial developments on their few migratory staging posts as from nuclear tests on their breeding grounds in the Arctic.

Of the long-haul migrants, pride of place must go not to a wader, though some come close, but to a seabird – the Arctic Tern. The terns, appropriately often given the popular name 'sea swallows' are perhaps the most graceful and elegant of seabirds, and are so delicate in structure that they seem unlikely contenders for such an energy-taxing title. Silver-grey and white, with darker wing-tips and black cap, a blood-red beak and long swallow-like tail streamers, they are smaller and much slimmer than any of the gulls. The Arctic Tern may well see more hours of daylight each year than any other creature. Many of them breed, as their name suggests, well north into the Arctic Circle where the summer months are virtually without darkness. Having raised their young on the short-lived summer abundance of insects, fish and plankton, they migrate southwards, crossing the Equator to spend the Northern Hemisphere winter in the Antarctic Ocean, right up to the margins of the pack-ice. Here again they benefit from the almost perpetual daylight of the Antarctic summer, and enjoy a similarly rich food supply.

During the breeding season Arctic Terns fish close inshore, flickering along lazily in the air a few metres above the waves before suddenly turning and plunging headlong into the icy water. Often these dives result in an audible 'plop' and a considerable splash, but the bird penetrates only a few centimetres rather than submerging deeply. The prey is almost always a small fish or a shrimp, which is taken back (one at a time, not by the beakful as does the Puffin) to the colony to feed the chicks. Early in the season the male will often bring a fish back to his mate, standing beside the shallow scrape that serves as a nest. Victorian ornithologists coined the term 'courtship feeding' for this action, inferring that (as in human society)

vary from 30 per cent to almost 100 per cent of the basic body weight, depending on the length of the migratory stages (or 'hauls' in aircraft terms) that the waders are undertaking. A simple analogy would be to regard the fat deposits as petrol in the fuel tank, ready for the journey ahead. Despite the hazards of human hunters, birds of prey, long overseas crossings and bad weather, quite clearly evolution and adaptation have seen to it that such migrations are worthwhile.

It remains to be seen whether the speed of 'progress' of mankind in the 20th century, and the pressure that industrial developments – ports, power stations, refineries, industrial complexes – are putting on coastal areas like estuaries in the industrialized countries of the temperate belt, can be catered for. Certainly, the environmental resistance to development in these areas, all too often regarded as wastelands in the planners' eyes, must now be increased not on a local scale but as a matter of national or, more often, international concern.

Many of the waders involved are very

Purple Sandpiper.

LEFT: Baird's Sandpiper.

PAGES 156–157: Whooper Swan – its musical trumpetting is evocatively echoed by the Finnish composer, Sibelius, in *The Swan of Tuonela*.

such 'gifts' reinforced the pair-bond between the two. Though this may be partly correct, at least as important is the pragmatic purpose that the 'gift' also serves. It is vital that the female be in as good condition as possible at the start of the season, so that her clutch (normally of two or three eggs) is as large as possible, with good-quality nutrients in the yolk, and can be laid soon after their arrival in the Arctic to take best advantage of the brief summer. She would find getting into top condition much harder without this feeding assistance from her mate.

Arctic Terns are colonial breeders, and the colonies may be thousands strong. Often they are located on remote beaches, or on small islands that offer a degree of protection from predators like the Ermine and Arctic Foxes, which have a taste for both eggs and chicks. Eggs and young are in addition magnificently camouflaged against the background of sand flecked with fragments of seaweed and shell. Although the colonies seem close-packed, which helps in the synchronization of the breeding cycle and in collective defence by vigorous attacks on intruders (that may even draw blood!), Arctic Terns are vociferously abusive neighbours, squabbling frequently. Closer inspection will show that the nests are always at least two beak-thrusts apart! The oldest Arctic Tern on record was a ringed bird that lived for twenty-six years. Travelling almost from Pole to Pole twice each year – a straight-line journey, with no deviations for fishing, of about 40,000 kilometres – its lifetime mileage is incredibly high, and certainly must have run into millions of kilometres.

Running a close second to the Arctic Tern would come the American Golden Plover. These have a simple but most impressive two-stage, south-ward migration in autumn. First they leave their Arctic tundra breeding grounds, gathering along the coasts of Nova Scotia and Labrador to feed avidly for the next stage, which is non-stop to their wintering grounds on the pampas of Argentina, travelling largely over the sea and crossing the Caribbean *en route*. Unlike the Arctic

LEFT: The Arctic Tern is one of the most graceful of all seabirds, and perhaps the furthest travelled. INSET: Arctic Tern with a sand-eel gift for its mate.

Tern, there is no opportunity for 'in-flight refuelling' by fishing at sea, if their pre-migratory feeding-up has not been adequate. The return journey, however, is made overland and in more gentle stages.

Particularly for the wildfowl and the waders, the timing of the northward migration is of critical importance. The Arctic summer is extremely brief, only just spanning a sufficient time for a large bird to arrive, lay eggs, raise young and get into satisfactory condition for the return journey south. Both at the beginning and at the end of the summer, the weather conditions are far from predictable and are often treacherous; even during high summer a blizzard always remains a possibility. Thus it is important that the arriving migrant in spring is in good condition, *and* carrying sufficient body fat both as insulation and as stored food to provide energy, as the chances are quite high that the breeding grounds will be covered in snow on their arrival.

To cope with situations like this, the American Golden Plover has its overland northward migratory route, but a wader like the Knot, wintering in southern Africa and breeding in northern Greenland, faces greater problems. The results of intensive ringing studies are beginning to reveal the Knots' solution: from South Africa to Britain, there are ample estuary stop-over areas, where food reserves can be recharged, but instead of leaving Britain for Greenland in a direct over-sea flight, the Knots seem to move, improbably, north up the coast of Scandinavia. This gives them an opportunity to assess the weather conditions and pace their migration accordingly, but in addition means that the final leg is made on a 'Great Circle' route from northern Norway due west to Greenland, minimizing the length of this stage flight and thus maximizing the fat reserves that the bird carries on reaching its breeding ground.

The majority of medium- and large-sized waders seem able to sustain their population numbers, despite the hazards (natural and man-made) on migration, and despite the uncertainties of the summer weather, with a clutch of four eggs. On occasions, the weather will be so bad as to result, over large areas, in the complete failure of the breeding season for many species, and of course time does not allow (as it does in more temperate latitudes) for the laying of a replacement clutch of eggs

Incubating female Golden Plover.

unless the disaster occurs right at the start of the breeding season.

Some of the smaller waders, still laying (as do the great majority of waders) a clutch of four eggs, seem to find this inadequate to sustain their population and have evolved some fascinating strategies to resolve this problem. An ideal example is provided by the Red-necked Phalarope. In some ways this is an atypical wader, in that it may winter well out to sea, rather than on the shore, and then it spends much of its time swimming buoyantly on the water. It often feeds on the water, using a needle-fine beak to pick small invertebrates like mosquito larvae from the surface layer. Frequently it will raise these food items from the muddy bottom of a tundra pool by spinning rapidly on the surface, creating a vortex, a miniature whirlpool, which sucks up likely food items from the bottom and delivers them to the waiting Phalarope at the surface.

Time does not allow the Red-necked Phalarope to follow the strategy of many songbirds from temperate areas of having two (or more) clutches of four or five eggs, laying and raising the young from the first, and then repeating the process. Around three weeks to a month of incubation, plus five or six weeks to raise the young to flying age and independent feeding, and the Arctic summer has largely gone: certainly insufficient time remains for the whole process to be repeated.

The Red-necked Phalarope shows another unusual avian feature in that the female is larger and more brightly plumaged than the male, and indeed it is she who takes the lead during courtship display. Having won her mate, she builds a nest with him, neatly hidden in the moss and rushes, and after they have mated several times, she lays a clutch of four eggs. These the male settles down to incubate – on his own, whereas in most other birds it is the female that bears the major brunt of this extended, dangerous and doubtless tedious task. Having set up one male to incubate the eggs and subsequently raise the chicks as a 'one-parent-family', the female moves off to entice another male – and this all in the space of a few days, so urgent is the need for haste – who, after pairing, is also left to raise her second clutch single-handed. She recuperates after her egg-laying labours, which sap a great deal of her reserves, feeding furiously prior to migration south again. In this way, the Red-necked Phalarope manages two broods of young in little more time than rearing a single brood would normally take.

Red-necked Phalarope spinning buoyantly.

The Sanderling, another of the smaller Arctic-breeding waders, is familiar to most birdwatchers in winter as a silver-grey and white wader that feeds on extensive sandy beaches, characteristically dashing in and out at high speed in between waves, snatching freshly disturbed prey from the surface. On their swift journey north from wintering grounds as far south as the Southern Hemisphere, the Sanderling moult into a beautiful, deep russet summer plumage, ideal camouflage among the tundra mosses, if not on sandy beaches. On arrival they pair up and mate in the normal way, but it seems that the female then lays two clutches of eggs in quick succession. (Double-brooded birds normally would lay the second clutch once the nestlings from the first had fledged). The male settles to incubate the first clutch, on his own and to rear them to fledging, while the female copes with the second. Again, two broods have been compressed into little more time than is usually taken by one.

In amongst the welter of wader-breeding

ABOVE: Sanderling. BELOW: Black Turnstone. The two Arctic-breeding Turnstones have short, shovel-shaped beaks, as their name implies ideal for turning over stones, and seaweed, in the search for insect prey.

On guard, but apparently
at ease: a Bean Goose on
the Northern European
tundra.

activity, the wildfowl too are getting their breeding season under way. Though not genuine wildfowl, the diver family are just as characteristic of tundra birds – Red-throated, Black-throated, Great Northern and above all the High Arctic White-billed Diver. Of all the bird calls in the world, those of the Great Northern and White-billed Divers must rate amongst the most thrilling, echoing wildly across the rocks and tundra around their breeding lakes. In North America the divers are called 'loons', and it is tempting to assume that this name is derived from the maniacal laughing in their song. A more likely origin is from the Icelandic word *lomr* which means lame, or clumsy. Divers are familiar birds to Icelanders, who would be well aware of their undoubted clumsiness on land.

In summer the White-billed Diver is as spectacular as its song: goose-sized, with a short neck and powerful white dagger-shaped beak, it is supremely elegant, the black head with a greenish sheen, the black back chequered with brilliant white squares. The body is extremely well streamlined, torpedo-shaped, with wings reduced in size. The feet are large, but rather than being fully webbed (like a duck's) have each toe fringed with semicircular lobes of skin. The legs are set back near the stubby tail for best propulsion – hence the divers' clumsiness on land, and their habit of only coming off the water to struggle the few metres to their nest.

Amongst the wildfowl proper, a great many of the geese are Arctic breeders. Of the grey geese, those breeding furthest north on the tundra include the Bean, White-fronted and

MAIN PICTURE: Strikingly white Snow Geese, characteristic of Arctic skies. INSET ABOVE: The Great Northern Diver produces the most haunting and evocative Arctic bird song/music *(Silvestris).*

ABOVE: A flock of Pink-footed Geese on Spitzbergen. These are temporarily flightless, having moulted their wing feathers.

RIGHT: Barnacle Geese – short stubby beaks indicate that their major food is short, fine grass.

Lesser White-fronted, and the Pinkfoot. It is the black geese, however, that are most characteristic. The Brent Goose, small, stubby-beaked and a specialist feeder on the marine grass *Zostera* during its winter sojourn on temperate estuaries, suffers the hardest summer conditions, breeding on several Arctic islands. So bad may the summer weather be that almost complete failures throughout the colony to raise any young at all during the season are not an unusual occurrence, and successful years, with most pairs of adults returning south with an average of two young, happen only once each decade. The Barnacle Goose, silver-backed and white-faced, does not suffer so severely from adverse climatic conditions in its breeding grounds, but more from the undesired attentions of Arctic Foxes as predators. To escape, many Barnacle Goose colonies are on cliff ledges, an incongruous nest-site for a goose, and one which though safe from predators, poses problems as the goslings leave the nest within hours of hatching – and are of course (unlike their parents) unable to fly! This problem is resolved by the goslings jumping to the tundra below: fortunately, dense down protects them against bumps on the rocks, and webbed feet broadly spread act, parachute-like, to slow their descent. Amazingly, most survive.

Dense down is a feature of Arctic wildfowl. Not only does it keep the adult birds warm, but when plucked from the duck's breast, provides an admirable nest-cup, insulated lining to protect the eggs from chilling. The Eider is famed for its down which fills duvets, eider-downs and parka jackets, and nest-linings are carefully harvested for this purpose in several Arctic areas. The duck Eider (and her counterpart in the King Eider) is magnificently camouflaged for her month-long endurance test as she incubates her clutch of eggs, leaving them only briefly to drink and occasionally to feed. In all the duck family, once mating has been successfully accomplished, the drake leaves his duck to carry the entire burden of raising the young. The fine plumage that he gained mid-winter, and it is spectacularly fine in the case of both

Steller's Eider rarely ventures south of the Arctic Circle.

Summer male Long-tailed
Duck.

the Eider and the King Eider, is used only during the display period, accompanied by musical crooning calls and much exaggerated posturing. Once the female is safely incubating, the drake moults into a drab, well-camouflaged, 'eclipse' plumage, to moult again into breeding-season finery at the end of the year.

Although there are many different ducks breeding within the Arctic, two others merit special mention. One is the Harlequin – as its name implies, with multi-coloured plumage. This is a specialist at living in coastal surf, and in streams made even faster-flowing over their rocky beds by the volume of summer melt-water. Harlequins spend much of their time in tight-packed flocks, moving with such synchrony that they seem to act as one. Harlequins dive for various aquatic and marine animals, usually small ones, and can manage to find a living even in the roughest water. Much the same is true of the Long-tailed Duck (or, delightfully, the 'Old Squaw' in North America). Small, active and musically vocal to an extremely well-developed degree amongst wildfowl, the male Long-tailed Duck is characterized by an extended and slim pair of central tail feathers, almost as long as the drake himself. The summer plumage is

largely dark brown, with rich buff markings and white patches: in winter it is the reverse, predominantly white with brown blotches. The Harlequin usually stays in Arctic waters year-round, whereas the Long-tailed Duck moves south to escape the severest weather – but no further than it needs.

Though penguins are normally absent from the Northern Hemisphere, and certainly from the Arctic, they do have a northern 'ecological equivalent' in the auk family. As with the penguins, though the auks are commonly thought of as polar birds, the majority of species come from appreciably more temperate areas. The adaptations of the auks to a marine existence are by no means so well developed as those of the penguins. They have a thicker than average subcutaneous fat layer, and their bodies are efficiently shaped for streamlining, particularly underwater. Auk wings are flipper-like in appearance, but they are still wings, and all auks can fly, certainly for long distances if not with much dexterity when it comes to landing in complex wind conditions (when it seems that most just close their wings, stop flying, and crash-land). They use their wings for propulsion beneath the surface, and it must be said that their anatomy suits them far better to an aquatic life than to a

Harlequin, a specialist
duck of river rapids and
coastal surf.

terrestrial or aerial one. They have an immensely strong 'box girder' composed of the breast bone, backbone and ribs, which protects the vital organs against the pressures of deep dives.

Most auks come ashore only for the breeding season, usually gathering in vast colonies. An exception to this is the Black Guillemot, which is in summer jet-black relieved by white wing patches and rich vermillion legs and lining to the mouth, and in winter the reverse, white with a few black markings.

Black Guillemots in summer.
In winter, they are largely
white and grey.

Black Guillemots occur in small groups, or even in pairs, and though widespread along Atlantic coasts, qualify as Arctic birds because they spend the whole year in many parts of the region. More exclusively Arctic is the Little Auk, or Dovekie.

In general terms, most members of the auk family are smaller than most of the smaller members of the penguin family, and no living auk approaches the King or Emperor Penguins in size. As its name implies, the Little Auk is small even among the auks, little bigger than a thrush, and unlike its relatives it feeds mostly on small crustaceans and plankton, rather than on fish. That said, it is an immensely successful bird, flourishing in its harsh environment. During the winter, Little Auks venture south, often not far beyond the Arctic Circle, and always staying in cold, food-rich waters. In spring, they move north to ancestral breeding sites, usually nesting in holes, often on cliff faces or screes, occasionally too in burrows dug in peaty soils. Numbers are massive, with many colonies estimated to be millions of birds strong. So numerous are they that they form a vital component in many food chains, preyed upon particularly by various members of the gull and skua families.

Of the gulls and the skuas, most are migrants, or at least are forced south to some degree by the winter. Two exceptions are Arctic specialists, the resident year-round Ross's Gull and Ivory Gull. Both are comparatively small and delicate for gulls, and both show polar adaptation by being relatively plump with shortish legs and a stubby beak,

The Little Auk is probably the most numerous of Arctic birds.

Little Auks or Dovekies.

The Ivory Gull, another
Arctic specialist rarely
travelling far to the south.

minimizing heat loss. Ivory Gulls nest in small colonies on rocky headlands as near, on land, as they can get to the North Pole. Nowhere are they numerous, and rarely do they venture much further south than the edge of the pack-ice. In a way akin to the Sheathbills of Antartica, they seem to obtain much of their food by scavenging, particularly around Polar Bear kills. They are successful though, perhaps rather more than other gulls of comparable size in much less hostile environments, as the average clutch of eggs is only two.

The Ross's Gull was for many years an ornithological mystery. Although early explorers had obtained specimens of this delightful bird, which is pinkish-white with a narrow black collar and very long in the wing in keeping with its buoyant, tern-like flight, it was almost a century before a breeding colony was found in 1885 in Greenland. In 1894, Nansen contributed further to Arctic knowledge of the bird, by locating several on the Franz Josef Islands, but not until the early 1900s did Buturlin describe a colony in detail.

Predatory birds in the Arctic are rather more varied than in the Antarctic. On the Low Arctic fringes are Great Skuas, almost indistinguishable in plumage and in habits from

Glaucous Gull: regularly winters outside the Arctic Circle.

their counterparts in the Antarctic, but not occurring in quite such harsh environments. Two other skuas flourish, especially when Lemmings are available in good numbers: the Long-tailed, slim and elegantly tern-like; and the Pomarine, altogether more robust and with odd, twisted, blunt central tail feathers. All function as outright predators, but also as pirates, harassing nest-bound auks, gulls and terns carrying food, terrorizing them so effectively that the food item is dropped in flight, to be snapped up in a marvellous display of flight skills, often before it touches the water. The Great Skua will even bully birds as large as Gannets, if necessary seizing and waggling the Gannet's wingtip as it flies, to force it to disgorge its fish.

In the far north the Peregrine (widespread though never numerous in the Low Arctic) is replaced by the Gyr Falcon, largest of all the falcons. Unlike the Peregrine, which often secures its prey in flight by 'stooping' – diving down on to it from a great height at speeds estimated to touch 200 kph on occasion – the Gyr, spectacularly white in some races, relies on sheer power and speed in level flight to overhaul and strike down its victim, which may be as large as a goose.

Both the white, spectacular Snowy Owl of the High Arctic and the buff Short-eared Owl of the Low Arctic are daylight hunters, gliding on stiff wings low over the tundra before pouncing on prey. Lemmings feature strongly in the diet of both, and Lemming numbers closely govern their breeding success. This adaptation goes some way to minimizing waste: in poor Lemming years the owls lay small clutches (sometimes not breeding at all), in this way reducing energy output and the risk of 'surplus' chicks dying.

As a further life-saving stratagem (though one abhorrent in human eyes), owls make good use of the fact that their eggs are laid at two- to four-day intervals, and that incubation starts as soon as the *first* egg is laid. In consequence, the owlets hatch at intervals, and in any owl's nest there will be seen a size-graded array of young, with the largest often substantially bigger than the smallest. Should there be a sudden disaster with the food supply and starvation threatened, then the largest owlet will eat the smallest, then the next smallest, and so on. In this way, brutal though it may seem, the chances of at least one youngster surviving are maximized.

Rough-legged Buzzards, too, are dependent on Lemmings for both clutch-size and distribution. Ground-nesters of necessity, they will shift their breeding areas to wherever Lemmings are numerous. In the specific name of the Rough-legged Buzzard, which is *Buteo lagopus*, once again the word *lagopus* occurs, the 'rough legs' (unusual in birds of prey) relating to the feathered tarsus and toes of the Buzzard, which serve to insulate the feet on snow.

Only the smaller birds, the song-birds or, more properly Passerines, remain for discussion. Unlike the situation in the Antarctic, there are several very attractive Passerines in the Arctic and penetrating well to the north. Of the most northerly adapted, the Shore (or Horned) Lark, the Lapland Bunting (or Lapland Longspur) and the Arctic Redpoll are all

LEFT: **One of the most elegant of Arctic birds, supremely acrobatic in flight, the piratical Long-tailed Skua.** BOTTOM LEFT: **Ross's Gull – an Arctic specialist rarely venturing south.** CENTRE LEFT: **Arctic Skua – another piratical predator-cum-parasite, occurring in dark (here) and pale plumage phases.** BELOW: **Arctic Great Skua – very similar, and closely related to its Antarctic counterparts.**

primarily seed or vegetable matter feeders. The other, the Wheatear (particularly the slightly larger, more colourful and more upright in stance, Greenland race) feeds predominantly on small invertebrates.

Wheatears breed in a broad belt through the Arctic, Sub-Arctic and cool-temperate regions of the Northern Hemisphere, right round the globe. Amazingly, all of them winter in tropical Africa, which implies some varied but always prodigious migratory feats for a bird little larger than a Robin. Those Wheatears from Siberia and Alaska fly overland, across Soviet Asia, down through the Arabian Gulf area and thence south into Africa. Those from Europe and European Russia migrate on a much shorter north/south axis, though this still represents a journey of several thousand kilometres. Those from Greenland and the adjacent islands were thought to make a major overseas hop to Britain, then travel overland into Africa, but it now seems likely, however much it strains the powers of belief, that some may fly direct from Greenland to North Africa. Certainly, from the amount of pre-migratory fat that these Greenland Wheatears deposit, often doubling their weight, such a journey is physiologically possible.

Appreciably paler and fluffier in plumage than its temperate cousins, the Arctic Redpoll breeds in the High Arctic – usually not nesting until June in scrubby tundra and dwarf willows. Seeds are its major food, augmented (as a protein source for the young) by such insects as are available mid-summer, and the Arctic Redpoll finds enough of them in areas of rock or tundra swept clear of snow by the wind to survive the winter in the High Arctic.

The Shore Lark, Lapland Bunting and Snow Bunting are all summer visitors to the rocks and tundra of the High Arctic. With no trees to act as song posts, they, like the Wheatear, must develop a 'song flight' for display, or in the case of the Snow Bunting, rely on the very strong visual signals produced by the striking black-and-white summer plumage of the male. Strangely, in its cool-temperate winter

Snowy Owl breeding success depends directly on small mammal numbers, as do most bird and mammal predator populations.

FAR LEFT: Wheatear – largely insectivorous, but successful in the Arctic and a long-haul migrant. LEFT: Lapland Bunting – or Longspur – handsome in the Arctic summer, but drab in winter plumage further south. BELOW: Peregrine: this high-performance, cosmopolitan, predatory falcon succeeds well in the low Arctic and its distribution goes as far south as the Falkland Islands.

RIGHT: Ptarmigan: well-adapted to survive the Arctic winter year-round, and well camouflaged.

FAR RIGHT: Well-fluffed feathers provide excellent duvet-like insulation for one of the most northerly of small birds, the Arctic Redpoll (*Hannu Hautala*).

Snow Bunting – splendid in 'worn out' plumage.

quarters, the Snow Bunting has its white colouration obscured by rich buff tones to the plumage – counter to the normal pattern shown in the Ermine, Hare and Ptarmigan, of a white *winter* coat or plumage being replaced by a more colourful, better camouflaged, summer one. Probably this is a case where the signalling value is of greater merit than camouflage in ensuring the Snow Bunting's continued survival.

Fascinatingly, the white summer plumage is obtained as the rich, buff plumage of winter wears out. This is not a case where the feathers are shed and replaced during a moult, but rather where long, dense buff fringes to the feathers gradually wear off as winter comes to a close, revealing the white feather bases beneath. Thus, at a single stroke of evolutionary progress, the Snow Bunting achieves the brightly-coloured summer plumage it needs for effective display, and loses much of the insulating quality of its winter feathers, a quality that could well result in overheating were not some evolutionary step taken to avoid it. Such closely-attuned adaptations – of immense variety – each achieved only with minute attention to energy conservation in so rigorous a habitat, are typical of the ways in which the birds of the polar regions have not only come to terms with their environment, but mastered it.

9
POLES APART

The two polar regions of the globe show a similarity in the icy grandeur of their scenery that might be expected because of the severity – even savagery – of their climates. They share a very brief summer of almost perpetual daylight, and a much longer winter, when days of crepuscular gloom lead into a period of unrelieved night. Temperatures may plummet to −50°C or below, the winds are searing and blizzards are frequent. Paradoxically, actual precipitation (as measured in centimetres of rainfall) is astonishingly low, creating (with the freezing temperatures removing much of the moisture from the air) an aridity unmatched in many typical deserts.

Ice and snow are everywhere. If there is rock, it is commonly shattered by frost and occurs in the form of unstable screes, not

PAGES 180–181: **The Valdez Oil Terminal in Alaska:** ecological protective measures failed disastrously when first tested by an oil spillage (*Steve McCutcheon*).

satisfactory as a basis for plant establishment. If there is soil, for many months during the winter it is deep-frozen, and even in mid-summer less than one metre below the surface it is frozen solid perpetually in the permafrost layer. This impedes the drainage of any summer melt-water, and creates the mires and pools familiar wherever there is tundra.

Such conditions create an environment that very few creatures and plants can tolerate. Survival in the polar regions demands adaptations of an extreme kind, but evolution has seen to it that these areas are by no means devoid of life. The various anatomical, physiological and behavioural stratagems that polar wildlife deploys in the mastery of its savage environment are collectively one major reason why these areas are so fascinating to mankind.

Considering the outward similarity of the two Poles, there are far more contrasts between their fauna and flora, and far fewer similarities, than might be expected. Though climatic conditions close to the actual Poles preclude continued life, not too far away conditions ameliorate sufficiently for the amazing picture to begin to unfold. All life

MAIN PICTURE: **Icebergs at Hope Bay in the Antarctic.** INSET: **Few regions can match the subtle lighting and colours of the Arctic icescape.**

owes its ultimate dependence for survival to plants, and in both polar regions there is a heavy preponderance of the so-called primitive plants: algae (sometimes single-celled), mosses and lichens, though whether 'primitive' is an appropriate adjective for a cooperative as complex and long-lived as a lichen is open to debate. Now, though, the contrasts begin to appear, for the North Pole has a comparatively rich higher flora, mostly of tundra plants. All of these are naturally enough stunted in their growth to avoid the worst of the climate, and show intriguing physiological adaptations, but many are as beautiful or more so in flower as their temperate or tropical counterparts. Such higher plants are almost absent from the Antarctic Continent itself, appearing (and then in nowhere near such an array) only on the Sub-Antarctic islands, many degrees of latitude to the north.

In invertebrate animal life, the story presents a close parallel to this, and in the same double dimension. Though there are many similarities in the more lowly forms of terrestrial invertebrates, for the insects at the upper end of the size scale once again the North Pole is far richer than the South. Even if it is nowhere near as richly populated with insect families as temperate or tropical ecosystems, the tundra shows to just what a degree a comparative handful of species – many of them blood-sucking flies, but including even butterflies and moths – can develop in the few short weeks of summer.

Marine life, be it the microscopic or near-microscopic plant and animal plankton, the fish, the seals, or the whales, provides the one example where the similarities exceed the differences. Although the actual species involved may differ, the entire structure of the marine ecosystem is much the same, and the adaptations – often extreme in the physiological sense – that have arisen are common to the marine inhabitants of both polar regions. As many of the whales are such long-range migrants, feasting on the summer richness of polar seas and retreating to temperate or even tropical waters for the months of winter hardship, for them this may not be too

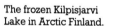

The frozen Kilpisjarvi Lake in Arctic Finland.

surprising. But the same argument cannot be advanced to account for the similarities in the plankton, or for that matter, for the seals.

The direct opposite is the case for the polar land mammals: the contrast between North Pole and South could hardly be more spectacular, as land mammals are absent from the southern polar region except where introduced artificially by man on the Sub-Antarctic islands. The Arctic mammals, both herbivores and carnivores, show fascinating adaptations to survival, and the 'King' of polar beasts, the Polar Bear, does actually venture on occasion close to the North Pole itself, normally the domain solely of seals and whales.

It might be expected that the birds, with powers of flight and navigational skills conferring an ability to migrate and exploit seasonal food supplies often thousands of kilometres from their wintering grounds which match or exceed those of the whales, might also show (as do the whales) perhaps more similarities between the polar regions than contrasts. This is not the case. The South Pole has relatively few bird species – just over forty of them and almost all seabirds. The great variety of the petrel family predominates, while the southernmost penguin species demonstrate the most extraordinary, the most extreme (and perhaps also the most successful) adaptations to polar life.

In the Arctic, the number of bird species exceeds the Antarctic total three-fold. The range of families represented is far wider. Although there are no penguins, the auk family fill that ecological niche (but with less extreme structural and behavioural adaptation). There are some petrels, but none is so extremely adapted as the southern species, probably because competition for food between species within the same family is not so severe. There are in addition many ducks, geese, swans, divers, birds of prey and owls, and even several small Passerines. These small songbirds are mostly seed-eaters, but include one, the Wheatear, that feeds mainly on insects and other invertebrates. All of these have mastered the conditions of the Arctic, at least seasonally; but the predominant group here are waders. With well-developed migratory and reproductive strategies, the waders dominate the tundra, and in terms of numbers of species, taken alone match the total avifauna of the Antarctic.

To seek such reasons as may be found for these disparities in polar plant and animal life, the origins of the two polar regions must be examined. Despite their 'equal-but-opposite' locations at the extreme ends of the globe (which in effect does little except place the seasons six months out of phase) and the similar (allowing for this lack of synchrony) severity and vicissitudes of their climates, there are some very striking contrasts.

The North Pole itself is located on a slowly-drifting, surprisingly thin sheet of ice, set in a comparatively small Arctic Ocean. Though this ocean may often be almost entirely frozen over, marine life can flourish beneath the ice. More important, the ocean is ringed by the Nearctic (North American) and Palaearctic (Eurasian) land masses, broken only by comparatively narrow sea channels. These land masses extend far to the south, through temperate to sub-tropical climates, so even for a land mammal, the opportunity to trek south to avoid the worst of the winter is always open. Looked at another way, a reservoir of potential Arctic colonists abounds close at hand, awaiting only the evolutionary opportunity.

In striking contrast, the South Pole is set on a major continental land mass, geologically of fairly recent origin in this location, as it is the product of the fragmentation of ancient Gondwanaland and subsequent continental drift. The Antarctic Continent itself is massive, occupying the bulk of the Antarctic Circle,

With time, the elements create fantastic sculptures from Antarctic icebergs.

and is composed of a rock base sheathed in an ice-cap often many thousands of metres thick. This huge, near-sterile continent is surrounded by the Antarctic Ocean, often (like its northern counterpart) covered in ice. The most important difference of all, perhaps, is that this ocean, often extremely stormy though rich in food, extends far to the north, with only the slender extreme tip of South America penetrating its vastness.

Dotted in a ring around the Sub-Antarctic are the islands and archipelagos which support much of Antarctica's wildlife, but these islands are few in number, generally precipitous, wet and windswept, and above all are small and extremely isolated from one another *and* from any major land mass that might act as a reservoir supplying potential colonists. It seems that it is this extreme isolation in a gigantic and stormy ocean which more than anything else accounts for the large differences apparent in the plant and animal life of the two polar regions. Where this physical contrast is immaterial, in the case of marine life including the sea mammals, differences between the two Poles are nowhere near so evident.

So far as mankind's associations with the polar regions are concerned, there are a great many similarities in the epic stories of exploration. Though in time the exploration of the Arctic has preceded that of Antarctica, over the centuries comparably ferocious seas, inhospitable land and a savage, unpredictable climate have combined to take a terrible toll in human life. Save for the survival skills evolved by the Inuit peoples in the Arctic, the polar environment is perhaps the only one that modern man has not mastered. He must be extremely careful that, in his greed for territory, for mineral or marine resources, and indeed even for scientific knowledge, the entire polar heritage does not go the way of whale populations, mutilated beyond recognition if not heading for extinction.

We have already seen the awful immediate impact of oil spillage on the marine birds and mammals off the Alaskan coast in 1989. Oiled Brunnich's Guillemots, Red-legged Kittiwakes and White-billed Divers present an unacceptable, pathetic and inhumane spectacle as they succumb to oil and cold: part of the already endangered Sea Otter population has

Booms designed to prevent the spread of oil spills proving ineffective after the shipwreck of the Exxon *Valdez* off the Alaskan coast (*Mark Newman*).

been eliminated. At present, we can only guess at the longer-term implications of this spillage. There is no doubt that man was at fault: a simple transgression of the rules of conduct in the oil industry, and of the rules of the sea, resulted in the shipwreck of a huge tanker. The warnings of ecologists; the care thus far taken in pipeline construction and in the exploitation of the Alaskan oilfield; the safety precautions and the training of personnel were all brought to nothing in moments. Worse still, confusion and inadequacy compound the unpreparedness of the authorities in attempting to limit ecological damage and remedy that which has been caused. It is to be hoped that lessons have been learnt from this dreadful example that in some way might mitigate the destruction which has taken place.

The polar regions of the Earth, despite their terribly harsh climate (indeed actually *because* of their climatic extremes) are delicate habitats. Any ecological damage, even so apparently trivial as tyre-tracks, may take centuries to repair, if indeed it is reparable. On nature's timescale, we are short-term tenants (with a full 'repairing lease') of the polar regions, not landlords anxious to extract the maximum rent in the minimum time. Mankind today is charged with ensuring the preservation for all time of these two spectacular habitats and the fascinating, amazingly well-adapted plants and animals that survive within them – poles apart.

Red-legged Kittiwakes – just one of the Alaskan animals to suffer from the spillage *(Glen Elison)*.

FURTHER READING

Research for the text of a book of this nature is a fascinating process. Such a wealth of material is available about the explorers involved, and about the polar regions themselves and their wildlife, that any suggestions as to further and wider reading must be very personally based. I am pleased to acknowledge the following books as being of major assistance. Not only was each a storehouse of information, but every one was an engrossing read, to be laid aside at the end of the evening only with difficulty.

Freuchen, Peter and Salomonsen, Finn.
The Arctic Year
PUTNAM, NEW YORK, 1958

Hosking, Eric and Sage,Bryan.
Antarctic Wildlife
CROOM HELM,LONDON, 1982

Miles, Hugh, and Salisbury,Mike.
Kingdom of the Ice Bear
B.B.C.,LONDON, 1985

Mitchell, Barbara, and Tinker, Jon.
Antarctica and its Resources
EARTHSCAN, LONDON, 1980

Rankin, Niall.
Antarctic Isle
COLLINS, LONDON, 1951

Reader's Digest.
Antarctica
READER'S DIGEST ASSOCIATION LIMITED, LONDON, 1985

Sparks,John, and Soper, Tony.
Penguins
DAVID AND CHARLES, NEWTON ABBOT, 1967

Stonehouse, Bernard.
Animals of the Antarctic – the Ecology of the Far South
PETER LOWE, LONDON, 1972

Sunset over Port Lockroy in the Antarctic.

INDEX